SEASONS OF LOVE

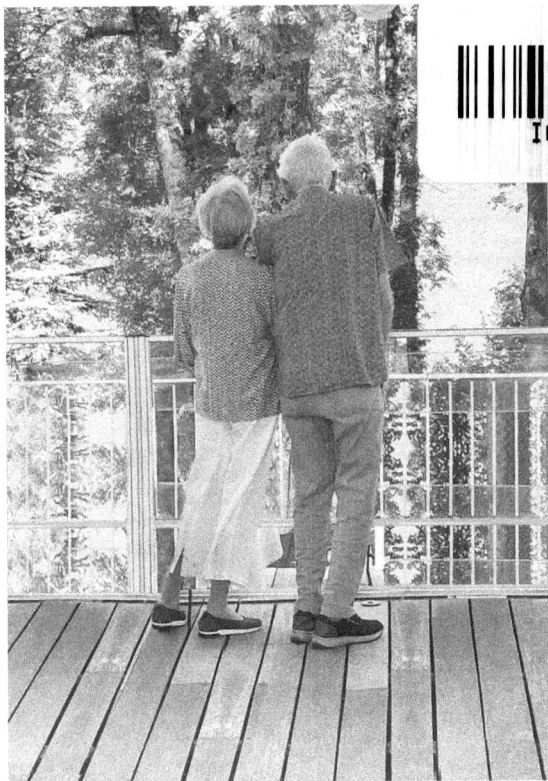

A LASTING MARRIAGE

Susan Marquardt Tiberghien

Author of *Writing Toward Wholeness,
Lessons Inspired by C.G. Jung*

CHIRON PUBLICATIONS • ASHEVILLE, NORTH CAROLINA

www.ChironPublications.com

Interior and cover design by Danijela Mijailovic
Printed primarily in the United States of America.

Front cover photo by Pierre W. Tiberghien

ISBN 978-1-68503-527-3 paperback
ISBN 978-1-68503-528-0 hardcover
ISBN 978-1-68503-531-0 electronic
ISBN 978-1-68503-529-7 limited edition paperback
ISBN 978-1-68503-530-3 limited edition hardcover

Library of Congress Cataloging-in-Publication Data Pending

Praise for *Seasons of Love*, Susan Marquardt Tiberghien

Reading *Seasons of Love* feels to me like being invited into a living prayer, the witness of two beloved companions across sixty-six years, bowing down 'before the uniqueness of the other.' Here the unfolding chapters of an unlikely and beautiful partnership merge fluidly with the rhythms and revelations of nature's own Art and Beauty. Beginning with a breathless kiss among a riot of azalea blossoms, Susan and Pierre teach us how to see and to admire our loved ones more intentionally, not least in the tension of opposites that, without love's tender embrace, might tear us asunder. Through it all, Susan's luminous prose teaches me to listen for the hidden God in the dance of all things, in all seasons, as the rush of young love and the joy of raising a family yields to the anguish of terrible family secrets and the physical limitations of aging. It is finally the voice of Wisdom-Sophia that I hear in these pages, inviting me in my own marriage, in my own solitudes, to trust in the seasons of love. For after every winter, this very special love story assures us, "there will be spring."

-Christopher Pramuk, Professor of Theology, Regis University, and author of *Sophia: The Hidden Christ of Thomas Merton*

For all who have struggled with the problem of marriage, this is a testimony to the potential sustainability of a committed relationship. Today, many people choose not to put their foot into these challenging waters, preferring career and the single life over marriage and family. Are they missing an important opportunity for individuation? Susan Tiberghien argues the case for marriage as the testing ground for the human capacity to love through thick and thin. Her story is a daunting achievement both in the living and the telling of it.

-Murray Stein, Ph.D., author of *The Mystery of Transformation*

Susan Tiberghien at 90 unrolls the extraordinary tapestry of her long marriage. This elegant writer, showing us the richness of love's power and shared commitment, opens up the challenges in growth. Readers will be left with a sense that love, like the earth, is full of endless surprises. And they will wonder if in their own lives, they could be more actively courageous in exploring the energies of partnership.

-Wallis Wilde Menozzi, Poet and Author of *Silence and Silences*

Susan Tiberghien's *Seasons of Love* takes us along as she recounts the setting forth on the always fragile barque of marriage, the entrustment of one's well-being with another. Her account reassures us that the venture is still worth the risk of caring for and being cared for by another, no matter what storms beset the voyage. At our last anniversary, a voyage now in its fifth decade, my wife gave me a card with one sentence printed on it: 'Someday you'll find this card in a drawer and we will still be in love.' Tiberghien's account, and that sentence from my deckmate, tell us that all the risk is necessary to arrive at the port-o'-call that first set us in motion.

-James Hollis, Ph.D., Jungian Analyst and author

This book is an ode to love and to relationship across the different phases of the arc of life. Written with soul and with courage, you will discover how family secrets can be lifted, how compassion and tolerance can heal, how deep understanding and the belief in a force that carries us can help us overcome trauma and find lasting love. Susan is a gifted writer, having lived herself a transformational process, her writing invites the reader to open up and let flow in the light. With a poetic and sensitive voice, she is also giving sensible testimony of both the highs and lows of 60 years of marriage. Inspiring, candid, captivating. You will not lay down this book until you have read the last page.

-Kristina Schellinski, Jungian Analyst, Lecturer and Author of *Individuation for Adult Replacement Children, Ways of Coming into Being*

Susan Tiberghien invites us into her marriage with Pierre from their very first kiss among the azaleas through 66 years together and gives new meaning to the vows "for better or worse, richer or poorer and in sickness and in health." Their marriage deepens through their immersion in two different cultures, anchored by their spirituality and the teachings of Carl G. Jung. Susan embraces the differences in their cultures as a way to harmonize the disparate elements of their psyches. She has the courage to reveal a family secret about sexual abuse and initiates a healing within the family for its blindness to the truth. She inspires us to trust that the seasons of marriage—"the cyclical and interconnected nature of life—bring serenity." She approaches old age with an acknowledgement of the physical challenges aging brings yet grounded in the abiding love she and Pierre share. Reading *Seasons of Love* you will be seduced by Tiberghien's words—poetic and inspiring—to experience the deeper meaning of love.

-Maureen Murdock, Ph.D. Author of *The Heroine's Journey and Mythmaking: Self Discovery and the Timeless Art of Memoir*

Susan Marquardt set sail from the U.S. for France in 1955, little knowing what this voyage would become. In *Seasons of Love*, she beautifully chronicles her ensuing journey of life accompanied by the man who would become dearest friend, companion and spouse: Pierre-Yves Tiberghien. Family, careers and diverse entailments soon followed.

Tiberghien's clear insightful prose artfully weaves the fates and challenges they encountered, amplified by reflections from C.G. Jung, Thomas Merton, Rainer Maria Rilke. It is the inspiring story of a relationship that grows ever stronger through encounters with the vicissitudes of life: inevitable twists of fate, vulnerabilities, forgivenesses and, most of all, Love.

-Robert Hinshaw, Ph.D., Faculty, C.G. Jung Institute of Zürich, Publisher, Daimon Verlag

For everything there is a season,
and a time for every matter under heaven:
a time to be born, and a time to die…
a time to mourn, and a time to dance…
a time to keep silence, and a time to speak…
Ecclesiastes

The love that consists in this, that two solitudes
protect and border and salute each other.
Rainer Maria Rilke, *Letters to a Young Poet*

Love 'bears all things' and 'endures all things.'
These words say all there is to be said.
Nothing can be added to them.
C.G. Jung, *Memories, Dreams, Reflections*

Seldom or never does marriage develop into an
individual relationship smoothly or without crises.
There is no birth of consciousness without pain.
C.G. Jung, *Civilization in Transition*

Table of Contents

Illustrations

Photos are credited to family members except Our Youngest at Phu My Hospice, Saigon, 1973 for which credit is unknown.

To Pierre-Yves, my spouse, partner, and dearest friend,
for sixty-six years
And to our children, grandchildren and great grandchildren.
Little did I imagine that in setting sail
for France at twenty-one years old,
I was setting sail for a life of lasting love.

Introduction

Pierre and I have been married for sixty-six years. We still savor the sweetness of a slow kiss, the warmth of the other's hand on one's back. We have both entered our ninth decade as we continue to celebrate the seasons of love. We who are so very different, not only in culture and language, but also in taste and temperament, what has kept us in love?

I grew up outside New York City, in a small family with one older sister, attending the Congregational Church most Sundays. Pierre grew up in northern France, in a very large family, the oldest boy with nine siblings, never missing one Sunday Catholic Mass. When we first met at university in Grenoble, it was the differences that attracted us. Like the childhood magnets I used to play with, the little white and black Scottish terriers, there are differences that attract and differences that repel. We are still learning to welcome the first and tame the latter.

In writing this book, I have looked back over the years, trying to glean hints about what went right. The seasons of our long marriage revealed themselves. First the spring. We fell in love with a kiss in the Villa Carlotta gardens near Bellagio on Lago de Como. Our courtship took us back and forth over the ocean. The kiss lingered.

The springtime of our love brought the births of five children in France, Belgium, Italy, and Switzerland, plus the arrival of a sixth who came to us from Vietnam. Everything seemed possible. We were caught up in the forward movement of our growing family.

The summer season found us more involved in our professional lives. Pierre traveled back and forth to the States for an American computer company and then returned to his first employer, the European Commission in Brussels. I found my way as a writer, publishing my first book, *Looking for Gold* for my 60th birthday. The children were in full blossom. Grandchildren were on their way.

Autumn came. We settled into our new home close to Lake Geneva. Pierre retired from his professional job and started to volunteer at a private foundation in Geneva. I continued to write and to teach both in Geneva and in the States. The fall colors were soon tossed about by strong winds and storms.

The winter of our love arrived. With it came still greater storms and the need to hold on to each other. We have found a fuller love, a love that survived adversity. A love that continues to deepen as we learn to let go and to appreciate the freshness of the present moment.

We want to remember Khalil Gibran words, "To wake at dawn with a winged heart and give thanks for another day of loving." We want each morning to say yes to his words. To rise in the morning wishing the other a new day of loving. Today we face my husband's Parkinson syndrome. We do not know from one day to the next how this neuro-degenerative disease will affect him, how slowly it will take hold of him.

If Pierre and I were asked what has made our lasting love possible, we would cite first courtship. To court and be courted, to seduce and be seduced. For years, this seemed natural. I courted him. I paid attention to how I looked. I asked the right questions. I made him feel appreciated, admired. I was seducing him. At the same time, he was courting me, paying attention to how he looked, asking the right questions, making me feel appreciated, admired. He was seducing me.

But courtship can lose its fervor. It needs to be renewed. It needs to be nourished. We used to dance together, wherever we could and often at home, just the two of us, especially to a tango. I like to say I fell in love dancing the tango. Pierre tangoed beautifully. I learned and followed. Now in the winter of our love, we still tango, less and less frequently, and more and more slowly. But we are together, side by side, moving with the music.

We have learned over the years which caresses give pleasure, which take us back to our first kiss in Bellagio, caresses which awaken our desire for the other. We remember the gardens at the Villa Carlotta, the deep pink azaleas, our closeness. We reach out to touch the other. We feel love's warmth. Sometimes we miss. We try again. Our lips remember.

Alongside courtship, we would cite commitment, our ongoing agreement to nurture our love every day. When we chose to pursue our lives together, we wanted the best for each other. We committed to "love and to cherish" each other. We wanted to embrace and endorse the goodness of the other. Our differences brought us together. However, with age we both have returned to our roots. Putting a traditional Frenchman and an innocent American together may offer romance but also discords. In cherishing the goodness of the other, the discords become stepping stones to a still deeper love.

I return to my childhood magnets, to finding the magnets which attract and amending those which repel. To experience our love as a continual coming together. C.G. Jung borrowed a word from the medieval alchemists to describe the coming together of opposites, a *coniunctio,* a conjunction whether it be in an alchemical furnace or in a relationship. In his last important work, *Mysterium Coniunctionis,* he wrote, "The factors which come together in the coniunctio are conceived as opposites, either confronting one another in enmity or attracting one another in love."

The opposites do not disappear, they do not dissolve. Instead, they continue to come together, to integrate, in a deepening wholeness, in the fullness of being. There is new growth. There is an opening to a new way of being. We think of the man and woman who come together, and the birth of their child. The man and woman stay side by side. There is no amalgam. Pierre and I have not lost nor even diminished our unique identities. Rather we have nourished our identities with each new *coniunctio,* bridging our differences to find new ways of expressing our love.

In writing about our love, I speak of marriage and relationship interchangeably, as I speak of spouse and partner. Pierre is both. Lover and best friend. As both he has helped me with this book. I want to know what he thinks, what he likes and what he likes less in my pages. In a deep way, *Seasons of Love* was written by both of us.

What is love? There are as many definitions of love as there are ways to love. We see our love as the force, the attraction, drawing us together. It is this force, this creative energy, that Pierre and I give to each other. Our love mediates between the two of us, honoring our uniqueness, our autonomy. It mediates also between us and our world, and ultimately between us and our creator.

I could have titled this book simply *Love*. But I wanted the title to recognize the seasons in love. Love is never stationary. I think of the well-known words of Heraclitus, "No man ever steps in the same river twice, for it's not the same river." The river flows always forward. It never flows backwards. Nor is it ever still. So is it for love. There are cycles of love that play out over the life of a marriage – spring, summer, autumn, winter. The same cycles play out also over each year of a marriage. Winter will always be followed by spring. Summer will give way to autumn. And the cycle will begin anew. Seasons within seasons, accustoming us to the cyclical nature of a long marriage. Indeed, the cyclical nature of all life.

Each year Pierre and I have experienced the different seasons of our love. There have been winters when our love has felt dormant. But spring has awakened us to the goodness of the other. There have been summers when our love has blossomed anew, Indian summers lingering into autumn when the leaves turn gold before falling to the ground. And the cycle begins anew. Year after year, and today after sixty-six years of marriage, it is extraordinary to find ourselves still in love. To reach for the other's hand and feel an inner warmth.

To look into the other's eyes and see a mirror reflecting our love.

To remember Khalil Gibran's words, "To wake at dawn with a winged heart and give thanks for another day of loving."

SPRING
Young Love

Pierre, Perugia, May 1956

Susan, Bellagio, May 1956

One Sweet Kiss

Our love story begins with a kiss and ends with a promise that our love will last. It will last as long as the kisses continue. I start our story with our courtship. Words from C.G. Jung in *The Red Book* guide me. *"Whoever is in love is a full and overflowing vessel. And awaits the giving."* To be overflowing vessels of love and await the giving, not the receiving. I stop and think about this. I want to be an overflowing vessel of love. Awaiting to give, not to receive.

Pierre and I have been courting one another for sixty-five years. Courtship is often defined as a period that precedes marriage. Instead, we see courtship as a period lasting as long as the relationship lasts. Or rather, the relationship lasting as long as courtship does. Courting is seducing. Jeremiah in the Old Testament cries out to Yahweh, *"You have seduced me Lord, and I let myself be seduced."* Jeremiah the prophet has been seduced by Yahweh. We can also use these words to describe our relationship to the one we love. We can seduce our partner and let ourselves be seduced.

One recent night, Pierre woke me. Something during his sleep had triggered his Parkinson. His legs were shaking, his back was shaking. I moved close behind him, my body holding him. He quieted and fell back asleep. I wanted this closeness to always be there for us. Warm memories of closeness—both physical and spiritual—filled me as I lay behind my sleeping husband.

I remembered our first kiss in the middle of azalea blossoms. We were on a student tour from the University of Grenoble to Venice. Pierre, an engineering student, was our guide. I was one of a group of foreign students. On the way back from Venice, across northern Italy, our tour bus stopped at Bellagio on Lago di Como. We took a boat across the lake to the Villa Carlotta where the azaleas were in full bloom. It was Pentecost weekend in mid-May with a full blue sky and bright sunshine.

We walked down shaded paths into a whirl of red, pink, and fuchsia azaleas. Somehow in the maze of all the blossoms, Pierre and I found ourselves alone. The bushes laden with flowers were taller than we. They opened their arms to welcome us, then closed them behind us. We were caught in an instant of longing. Pierre bent down and lifted up my face. Still today, I taste the sweetness.

After that first kiss at the Villa Carlotta, we spent long moments together back in Grenoble at the University. Only one month remained before I was to return to the States. We had met in the fall at the beginning of that university year. I had arrived on a graduate fellowship to study 20th century French literature. Pierre was in his third year of engineering studies.

I backtrack to our first meeting: Shortly after my arrival in Grenoble, I attended a welcoming evening for foreign students at the Cercle Universitaire International. It was upstairs in one of the university buildings, up a narrow flight of stairs to a room in the attic. At the top of the staircase, Pierre was waiting to welcome me. I close my eyes and see the staircase. I see Pierre at the top. So began the prelude to our love story.

Our friendship deepened during the winter months. We pursued our different studies—Pierre in engineering, I in French literature—often finding each other in the same group of friends in the evening. There was less pairing off in couples in France than in the States. We remained a group of three girls and four boys most of the year. In January an extraordinary set of circumstances foreshadowed my future. Pierre's sister, my age, died of early lung cancer. One of Pierre's friends asked me to accompany him in driving Pierre home, a three-hour drive through the Alps to the city of Annemasse, close to Geneva. And then to keep him company returning together to Grenoble. It was late evening in a blinding snow and ice blizzard. The car slid into a ditch. We found a telephone in a café where a light shone behind the closed shutters. Pierre's father came to pick us up.

Pierre's mother, surrounded by children—several of his seven younger brothers—greeted us at the front door. Pierre, his friend, and his father went upstairs to Christine's room to pray and watch over her. His mother saw that I was stricken with apprehension. She offered to take me to a bed where I could rest for the night. The bed was in a small laundry room tucked under the staircase. I remember piles of white bedding and nearby on the floor rows of black shoes waiting to be polished. Why was I so afraid? Death had taken his sister's life a few hours earlier. Where was God? The storm thrashed against the window. Footsteps went up and down the staircase to Christine's bedroom. It was my night to wrestle with Jacob's angel.

In the morning Pierre knocked on the door. The family was gathering for breakfast. The storm had passed. Sunlight poured into the room. Outside everything was white, pristine, under a blue sky. Somehow my trust, my faith in God, in all will be well, was restored. I joined the family in the large dining room and gave grace in my heart.

Our relationship took on a different tone. Who was this person I was getting to know? What was bringing us together to talk about death, about the death of his sister, the death of someone my age? I was looking for answers, interrogated by the constancy of his faith, in wonder of his family who welcomed a stranger the night that the angel of death passed through their home.

The weeks and months passed. We continued to find moments together in the midst of our classes and friends. Then came the student trip to Venice ending with our first kiss in the gardens of the Villa Carlotta across from Bellagio, on Lago di Como. Our friends saw that something had changed. We thought we gave no signs of our nascent love, but our friends said it was the way we looked at each other. I would like to think that this is still true today, that our love radiates in our eyes.

Back then we wondered, would we always look at each other this special way, with rainbow-tinted glasses? Would I always see Pierre so attractive, so appealing? Would I always see him in such favorable light? What was ahead of us? We grew up on different sides of the ocean. We spoke different languages. We bathed in different cultures. Even our studies and interests were in different fields. How would our respective families respond? Neither of them had travelled to the country of their intended in-law. Each of us was a foreigner for the other's family.

We decided to give our nascent love a chance. We would continue our courtship through letters. We chose a book to read and discuss in writing. We chose Thomas Merton's *Seven Story Mountain*. We read it in French, *La nuit privée d'étoiles*. The choice was prescient. As Thomas Merton found his way to becoming Catholic and entering the Trappist monastery Gethsemani, so would I find my way to becoming Catholic and entering Pierre's family. Our separation that first year, instead of taking us down different paths, brought us closer together on adjoining paths.

There was an early coming together of our minds and hearts. C.G. Jung called this union a *coniunctio*, a conjunction. As I wrote in the Introduction, Jung borrowed the word from the medieval alchemists to describe a coming together of opposites, whether it be in an alchemical furnace or in a relationship or elsewhere. The opening sentence of his last major work, *Mysterium Coniunctionis*, reads, "The factors which come together in the coniunctio are conceived as opposites, either confronting one another in enmity or attracting one another in love." In a relationship, together in love, each one keeps his identity, his autonomy, while creating a unity of shared interests.

I think of my childhood magnets. They were little plastic dogs, black and white Scottish terriers. They either attracted each other or repelled each other. Our lifetime of love has been the story of these magnets. We have tried to nourish the ones which attract and tame the ones which repel. I see my little terriers standing side by side with their heads up. Marriage is one long *coniunctio*. So I see Pierre and me, now in our ninth decade, standing side by side. We are still learning to keep our heads up. Our differences have deep roots. Their tenacity reveals itself more strongly as we age.

I grew up Protestant in a small family, with one sister, in Briarcliff Manor, a village in the outskirts of New York City in Westchester County. Pierre grew up Catholic in a very large family, with nine siblings, in Tourcoing, a city in northern France. Our cultures and languages were literally an ocean apart. When we met at the University of Grenoble, I was a young graduate student studying contemporary French literature. Pierre was finishing an engineering degree in electro chemistry. I was interested in words. Pierre was interested in numbers. I could continue down a long list of opposites. Yet we were falling in love.

We wrote our letters in French. It was the language of our meeting and of our courtship. As it would be the language of our lovemaking. Writing in French slowed me down. During that year's separation, while reading together *The Seven Story Mountain*, I took my time each week to spend an evening writing to him. I imagined him sitting close to me, his gray eyes watching me, waiting for my words.

Courtship through letter writing—describing my days, my daily commute to the city for work at Macmillan Publishers, a bike ride over to the Hudson River to watch the sunset, games of bridge with my sister and parents. He wrote about the last year of his engineering studies, his work in the national student union, his holidays with his family in their chalet in the Alps. We shared passages of *Seven Story Mountain*, passages that spoke to us and also those that troubled us. It was a way into the mind and heart of the other.

It was also an introduction to my later reading of Thomas Merton. In my writing and teaching, I often speak of two walking sticks, Thomas Merton and C.G. Jung. It was in my fifties that I turned back to reading Merton. It was at a time when I was questioning my faith. Merton gave me answers. At the same time I was starting to read the work of C.G. Jung. I have held on to my two walking sticks as I continue to uncover my deeper self. Pierre has learned to step aside by moments as I enter anew *The Journals of Thomas Merton* or *The Red Book* of Jung. I always come up to rest in my husband's arms.

In July, after a year's separation, I flew back to France. I wanted to see if I could imagine living with him in France. Would I still feel the deep love attraction? Where would we live? We never had spoken about this. It just seemed a given to live in his country. He did not know my country. My one year at Grenoble had shown me that I adapted easily and happily to a French speaking and thinking milieu. I had met his parents, first in the exceptional circumstance of the death of Christina, then again for a short visit in the summer before returning to the States. But would they welcome me as their first daughter-in-law? They, a very traditional Catholic

French family from Tourcoing in northern France, and I, a candid young American, Protestant by faith.

My parents understood my love for Pierre. He had won their affection during the summer after our year in Grenoble when he had an internship at General Electric in New York. He spent the weekends in our home where we were discreetly chaperoned. My parents could have discouraged me, hoping to keep me on their side of the ocean. Instead they saw my happiness, my love for Pierre. As I think back, it was remarkably unselfish of them. Their love and support were a constant in my life.

There was still another reason for my return to France. I hoped to find a way to finalize my decision to enter the Catholic Church and to take this step away from my hometown. My years in an Episcopalian boarding school followed by my studies of philosophy at university had set me on a quest for something mystical, undefinable, approaching the holy—something I did not find in the Congregational Church of my family. I wanted to follow my longing for the numinous. My wrestling with Jacob's angel the night of Christine's death coupled with the slow reading of *The Seven Story Mountain* by Merton had led me toward the Catholic mystics, to reading Saint Teresa of Avila and Saint John of the Cross. I had asked for instructions at Maryknoll, the Catholic monastery in Ossining, close to my home. I felt ready to embrace the Catholic faith. I wanted to do so far from my small hometown church where our family was prominent. My decision concerned only me.

I flew to Paris and traveled by train to Grenoble where Pierre was doing his military service. I still can picture the rolling green countryside, the tucked away villages, mandalas with church steeples in the center, the Alps rising in the distance. As the mountains came closer, I stared out the window. It had been so long since I last saw him. Soon he would be in front of me. What would I feel? Would it be the same? My friends questioned me. Why a Frenchman? Surely you're not serious. Surely you're not going to go live in France! I only smiled. I did not have the answers. I only knew I was in love.

The train slowed down, then stopped. I stood up, reached for my suitcase and walked to the door. Pierre was waiting on the station platform. We rushed into each other's arms. Stunned, we stood there close together, until we were the last to find our way to the street. Six weeks later, we were engaged.

French Housewife

That same summer, now 66 years ago, my wish to embrace the Catholic faith was realized. I was welcomed into the Catholic Church by a Swiss Dominican priest, Father Jean de la Croix Kaelin, in the French mountain village of Samoëns where Pierre's family has a chalet. That day in the middle of the French Alps, the sky did not open. There was no glorious burst of light. Indeed, it was raining. But I felt sheltered and safe in the walls of the ancient church thousands of miles from my own home. How this would change. The walls would shake. But I am skipping head. I return to the early spring of our love.

We had less than a year to court one another before our marriage. Pierre was in New York City at Columbia University studying for an MBA. I had left my job in publishing and was teaching at a high school near my home in Briarcliff. We spent our weekends together. The months passed as we prepared for our marriage. I think of the story of the Petit Prince, where the fox tells the little prince that one needs to prepare one's heart before welcoming a friend. We were welcoming the other into a life-long relationship, into a life-long commitment to love one another "until death do us part."

Spring vacation came. We were married on Easter Monday in the Church of the Magdalene in Pocantico Hills near my home, with both a Catholic priest and a Congregational

29

minister receiving our vows. We had a Catholic marriage ceremony without the Mass but with shared prayers and readings from the two traditions, read by both priest and pastor. We were bringing together our different childhood faiths. We stood side by side as we made our vows facing the two representatives of the Christian faith. Pierre's parents and two of his brothers were with us from France, along with my parents and my sister and brother-in-law. There were our friends from both countries, and many of my students from the school where I was teaching. It was our little world come together to celebrate our love.

We had just one week of school vacation for our honeymoon in a quiet hotel in the blue mountains of Virginia. One week to make love. There was reciprocal joy and delight as we discovered each other's nudity. We were both prudish, taking our time, listening carefully to one another, looking intensely into the other's eyes. Still today, we have warm blissful memories of this short honeymoon. Our bodies found their way to each other in a deepening mutual trust.

We continued to court each other. Surprising the other with a warm kiss on the cheek, or a longer kiss on the lips. Reaching for his hand in the middle of the night. All the innumerable little ways of courtship. Doing things we know the other likes. Daily habits that kept us attractive to each other. Courtship. Looking for ways to make myself attractive to Pierre. I often asked him about how he saw me. I wanted to learn his tastes and make myself attractive and appealing. I still do. Likewise, I wanted him to look good. To look good for me. To attract me, to make me want his arms around me. I wanted him to also look good for everyone else. I was proud to be his partner.

Pierre received his MBA from Columbia, I finished my teaching, and we took summer vacation to cross the country in a Nash Rambler, with a mattress in the back. We drove for over 20,000 miles, finding campgrounds for the night, and every few nights a motel for a shower and more comfortable bed. I think back and realize how this adventure gave us a complicity which is still ours today. When the universal joint in our car fell out for the third time as we were climbing into the Sierra Nevada mountains in Arizona, all we could do was hope a good Samaritan would stop and drive us to a garage. We made it back to my parents' house, having discovered the good Samaritan and the extraordinary breadth of my country, with a car on its knees.

Then off we sailed to France. I packed a steamer trunk with my belongings. It was time to wave goodbye to family, friends, and the USA. Ahead of us was Pierre's military service, two years and a half in the air force. It was in 1958 during the French Algerian war. Pierre would go to officer training in the air force. If all went well, he would be able to choose a specialization that avoided active duty in Algeria.

I moved into his parents' home in Annemasse in the French Alps, there where I had arrived in the middle of the stormy night close to three years earlier. Christine's bedroom on the third floor of their large house was now my bedroom. In many ways I was taking her place for my parents-in-law. I was unaware at the time that I was accepting this role. The effects of this replacement held me captive in the persona of someone I never met. It was many years later that the insight of a dear friend and Jungian analyst identified my role as a replacement adult.

This brings me to write about synchronicity. With age I am more and more aware of this connecting link to an invisible matrix. Meaningful coincidences abound in our lives, they surround us if we pay attention. They have no rational explanation. They are acausal. A person has a thought or a dream that coincides with an event. I dream of my youngest granddaughter, and the next day she stops in to say hello. Or two different events coincide for no apparent reason. I am reading a certain book when a friend calls to say she has just discovered a book that she wants to share with me. It is the same book that I am reading.

Such happenings point to an underlying connecting principle, a pattern of oneness, in the deeper level of the unconscious which Jung named the collective unconscious. We are connected to one another interpersonally. These happenings are not pure chance. They are the manifestation of our oneness. As Jung wrote, "Synchronicity is an ever-present reality for those who have eyes to see." Today, the view of reality as an interconnected cosmic web in which the observer is an essential participant is fundamental to quantum physics. The dots are connecting as creation continues to evolve.

It was synchronistic that one of my close friends would herself be a replacement child who would lead me to understand that I was a replacement adult. I was replacing Pierre's sister, living her life which was cut short by her death. My own potential was held in check. Only with time would my Jungian studies, coupled with a practice of silent prayer, open the way to uncovering my own deeper self.

In this story of our love, there is an earlier awe-inspiring synchronicity that brought me to the house of my future family-in-law the night that Pierre-Yves' sister died. There was no rational explanation for my presence in his home that evening. I was simply asked to accompany his friend as he drove Pierre-Yves home. It is to note that my arrival that night did not go unnoticed in Pierre's family. His mother, after our engagement, shared with me a letter from her father, Pierre's grandfather, in which he wrote, "The night the Lord took Christine, He gave us Susie." Pierre's grandfather was unknowingly seeing synchronicity through his Catholic faith.

This letter reveals also the name by which I was known—am still known—in France. It was at Grenoble that people called me Susie. I do not know why. But I do know that from midlife onward I no longer liked being called Susie. I did not feel like "Susie." I felt like "Susan." In my thinking, the two names designate very different people. I have tried to win back "Susan," but the French do not like this word, they do not know how to pronounce it. It's either SU-sie or SU-zanne, with the tonic accent on the SU. Still today I am Susie for my French friends, my French family, and yes for my dear husband. I sometimes turn around to see whom they are calling. Who is she? Where is Susie?

I lived for six long months upstairs in Christine's bedroom. Fortunately for my outgoing nature and peace of mind, I found interesting work in the public lycée as a foreign assistant, teaching English to the last year students preparing their Baccalaureate. I enjoyed the challenge and again found enjoyment and fulfillment in teaching. Pierre succeeded in his officer training and chose to specialize in air control at the Orly airbase, south of Paris. I was able to join him. "April in Paris." We were together again, young lovers in Paris. We were finding our way between two countries, two cultures, two languages. Each day a *coniunctio,* a conjunction, a coming together. And soon there would be our first child. My playful childhood magnets were happy.

In the summer we headed south. Pierre was assigned to the prototype testing airbase at Istres, not too far from Marseilles. For the next year and a half he would work three days and nights at the control tower, guiding planes safely up and down. Then be off for three days and nights. I was duly impressed that in six months he had learned enough to direct the pilots to land and to take off. All the more so as it was a prototype testing airbase, the pilots must obey the air control officers.

Overnight I became a French housewife, a metamorphosis. The closest American it seemed was the wife of the mayor of Arles eighty miles away. There were latent reservations in the area about Americans which dated back to the Second World War when the region accepted the Vichy regime and resisted our troops. I felt this in my daily interaction with the merchants in the open-air markets and in the shops. My accent gave me away and often caused glares if not grimaces.

We were renting the ground floor of a family home. I made friends with my next door neighbor, Madame Michelle, an imposing widow with a domineering bosom. We had no heat in our apartment, and it happened to be the coldest winter in many years. The Curé even sent us home from church one Sunday without Mass, saying it was too cold. I was awaiting our first child. Madame Michelle came to my help and insisted that the owners install a wood furnace. Then she helped me learn how to light the fire and make sure it would keep burning.

Little Pierre was born that winter. My gynecologist, a fervent card carrying Communist, was persuaded that with Pavlov training, childbirth should be painless. I had undergone the training. But after long hours in the private Pavlov birthing room at the hospital, he gave up and handed me over to the midwife in the general ward. He blamed it on my nationality. I was too American. The midwife hoisted herself up on the flat bed and pushed the baby down and out. Pierre was waiting outside in the hall. The births of our other children were easier. Pierre was always at my side. However in 1959, this was not allowed in the hospital at Salon de Provence even if the expectant mother was trained with Pavlov's painless child birth.

During our time in southern France, we joined a group of couples at the church. The group was part of the Equipes Notre Dame, the Teams of Our Lady, a movement started in Paris after the Second World War by several couples looking to live their faith as husband and wife. Under the guidance of Abbé Caffarel, they set up teams of five or six couples, following a program for conjugal spirituality: prayer, reflection, retreats, a rule of life. The movement took hold and spread quickly in Europe and then around the world. It continues to provide support to married couples in over ninety countries worldwide.

The five couples in our team in Istres were all French, as was the chaplain. For most of them, I was the first American they had met. It was here that Pierre and I learned about the "sit-down," a monthly sitting down together, husband and wife, to reflect upon their relationship—what was working well, what was working less well. The idea comes from the Gospel of Luke, where it is mentioned that before building a tower, one needs to sit down and count the bricks. "For who among you, intending to build a tower, does not first sit down and count the cost, whether he has enough for the completion." Luke 14:28

This was the beginning of our monthly couple dates. We would have a quiet evening at home, or an evening at a restaurant, a time to listen carefully to one another. We would review where we were in our daily life, where we were with each other, and where we were with those around us. Our couple dates were monthly coming togethers to refresh our relationship. Sometimes we forgot the monthly date. Other times we did not want to sit down together. Seeds of discord would be lifting their heads. We learned to wait until we were ready anew to listen to each other

As Pierre's military service in southern France was drawing to a close, he answered a job offer in the French newspaper *Le Monde,* for an engineer at Euratom, the European Nuclear Research Agency in Brussels. Pierre jumped on the opportunity, wanting to work internationally. He felt strongly that a united Europe was essential for world peace. Too often Germany and France had confronted one another on the battlefields. He was awarded the job. We set our vision on Brussels and more importantly, on one Europe.

Pierre junior, soon called Peter, was growing into an independent little being who knew what he wanted. In the mornings we went to the market together. I had picked up the French habit of daily shopping in open air markets. In the afternoons he and I would join his father at the airbase. I'd take his pushcart and we'd go for a walk along one of the runways not in use. In the early evening I'd put him to nap and sit down to play bridge with Pierre and two sergeants in the control tower. We were never certain this was allowed: me in the tower or the three of them playing cards.

Pierre Junior at the Airbase in Istres, France

November arrived. We said goodbye to our friends in the Team and in the control tower. It was time to pack our car, a *deux-chevaux*, with our few belongings. When Madame Michelle came to see us off. She wiped away tears. "I never had a neighbor before." It was my turn to cry.

More Babies

I was expecting our second child for the spring. Unaware of the linguistic division in Brussels between the French and the Flemish, we had rented an apartment in the Flemish speaking part of Brussels. Upon arrival, we hunted down the Equipes Notre Dame and were placed in a team of five couples, mostly lawyers. All of them had studied at Louvain University. All of them were proud parents of two or three toddlers. Our new friends took us in hand, found us housing in the French speaking part of the city, led me to a gynecologist who was also the Queen's gynecologist and therefore not a Communist trained in Pavlov's painless childbirth. Very soon they were giving us lessons in how they were raising their children.

Pierre and I were grateful. Instead of confronting one another about how to bring up our children, we listened. We were raised so very differently. How would we raise our own children? A nanny and then a tutor took care of Pierre as his mother gave birth to eight more siblings. Children did not talk at the dining table unless they were asked a question. The one authority, his father, the patriarch, was never questioned. It was another world from my sister's and mine where there were few rules, where our mother encouraged us in all we did, and our father played kickball with us after supper on the road in front of our house.

As I write this, I see how the Teams were a way for us to grow together. Already when we lived in southern France, they helped us find a middle road in our faith practices. Now in Belgium they were helping us find a middle road in bringing up our children. The compromises brought our opposites together. And each time the compromise brought new growth, deeper love and more babies. *Coniunctios*!

Pierre reveled in his work. His studies as an engineer and the business courses at Columbia trained him for managing different research projects. He was with colleagues who shared the same aspirations for a strong united Europe. I was happy to find volunteer work teaching English at an international student foyer affiliated with the University Libre de Bruxelles. It was here where I found our first babysitter, a Tunisian student. For our 20th wedding anniversary, he invited us to his small hotel on the island of Djerba. He took us to the annual enactment of the landing of Ulysses on the island. We sat on the beach and watched as the ancient boat arrived. The gifts of friendship.

We were happy to welcome several of the foreign students for meals at our home. It was this way that we got to know a Chadian student finishing his doctoral degree. He had literally watched the rebels burn down his home in Tchad during the first civil war in the early 1960's. Being on the losing side, he had fled his house just in time and was now exiled. He would not return to Tchad except to find his wife. They settled in the Ivory Coast where we were able to visit them in Abijean. He came to stay with us for a visit when we were living in Italy, then again when we were in Switzerland. Another celebration of friendship.

With Pierre's contacts at the European headquarters and my foreign students, our world was full and varied. Our two children were soon to have either a baby brother or sister. To help me at home, I found a 'fille au pair,' a mother's helper from Wales, the first of many who would follow one another as our family continued to grow. And who would free me so that I could continue my part-time teaching.

After four years in Brussels, Pierre was assigned to a research center in Italy, in the village of Ispra on Lago Maggiore where Euratom was building a nuclear research reactor. Over seven hundred scientists and engineers were involved in the project. Pierre was part of the management team for the construction. We found housing in the small village of Comerio, halfway between Ispra and Varese, an hour north of Milano. I was back in a village where there were no other Americans. But this time I was warmly welcomed as "la mama americana" of three small children. Italians love their bambini.

Our apartment was in a small building, really a large house, with four apartments, up a narrow one-way lane on a high hill overlooking the village and in the distance Lago Maggiore, the Italian Alps, and Monte Rosa. Beyond our house were dense woods where hunters came each September. At the bottom of the hill lay the village cemetery. Across the street, the village church. Bells rang out four times a day. Often I went to weekly Mass. Women sat on one side of the church and men sat on the other, or rather they stood outside the main door. A woman would drape a white kerchief on my head when I went to the altar for communion. For Sunday

Mass we went with the children to a French speaking service in a church close to the research center at Ispra.

There were no Teams waiting to welcome us. Instead, along with an Italian couple who had been in a Team in Rome, we started one of the first teams in northern Italy. We easily found four other couples with husbands working at the center, all fluent in French, and a willing Italian chaplain. It was a stimulating group of different European nationalities, all of us raising children, all of us committed to a united, peaceful Europe.

The children went to the European school in Varese. These schools were created by the European Commission in the five original member countries: Belgium, Germany, France, Netherlands and Italy. The UK joined the Commission only in 1973. I accepted a part-time teaching position at the school to teach religion. The curriculum offered a choice: a class in religion or a class in ethics. I tried to teach both in my class.

We soon welcomed our fourth child. He was born in Italian. Not simply in Italy but in Italian with an Italian doctor who spoke no English, no French. It was a difficult birth for the child and for the mother. We stayed in the hospital through the Christmas holiday as the baby remained for several days in an incubator. We finally came home without the bottle of oxygen that the Catholic sisters wanted us to take, just in case. Our son was fine.

We were living up a hill without a telephone. It took three years for the local phone company to string telephone wires up the hill. I used to run down the lane, when necessary, to use the pay phone in the village café. So it was one morning

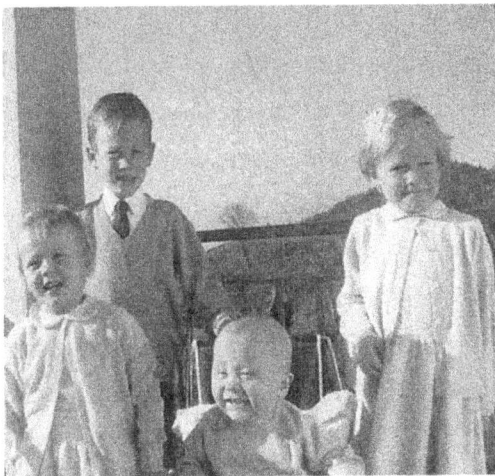

Our Four at Home, Comerio

when I woke and found the two girls covered with red spots. I looked into my Dr. Spock book and detected scarlet fever. Down I ran to telephone to our Italian pediatrician. He arrived in the afternoon, honking his car all the way up the hill in case someone was coming down.

Dr. Spock was right. The doctor explained that usually scarlet fever required hospitalization in Italy, but if the girls were strictly quarantined, he would agree to let the girls stay home. The older brother would be kept home from school for two weeks. And oh, the baby. I was to keep him isolated from everyone. We all survived, including the relieved Italian baby doctor.

The children were happy in their European school and happy at home where they played most of the time outside on the terraced hillside. Pierre drove to work each day with our neighbor. I enjoyed my afternoons of teaching at the European school. We continued our participation in our young team and helped start other teams in the region. Italian women welcomed the Teams which helped them start carrying their weight in their marriages.

Everything seemed possible. Pierre and I both felt there was room for a fifth child in our already large family. It was the time of Vatican II. In the Catholic world, hopes were high for reforms, for opening the walls of the church to women, to oecumenism. Changes did happen. The Mass was celebrated in the local language rather than Latin. The altars were turned around, and the priest faced the congregation instead of the altar, showing only his back. But these changes were minor. There was still no place for women in the clergy, still less in the ruling body. And the door to a more inclusive oecumenism remained closed. Finally, the new papal decree Humanae Vitae outlawed birth control.

This did not pose an ethical problem for me. I had never accepted the stringent rules and regulations of the Catholic Church. Pierre leaned in my direction. We had found our way for birth control using the temperature readings each day. With careful readings we were able to plan for each new child. It is extraordinary today to remember back to when and where each new life was conceived. Our shared spiritual life was an important part of our relationship, contributing toward our togetherness.

Grateful to the Teams, we were happy to help the new Teams in the region, to liaise between them and the center of the movement in Paris. We were both committed to giving back to this organization some of what they had given us. We traveled to visit other Teams in Italy. We had done this earlier as liaison couple for the Teams in the States, flying to New York and across the States visiting the teams recently implanted. The friends we made in America and in Italy, and still earlier in Belgium and France, have stayed with us. We all shared a sincere desire to practice our faith as married couples and contribute together to a just and peace-loving world.

For number five, I left Italy behind and found a French speaking gynecologist across the border in Lugano, Switzerland. The birth arrived on time. My stay in the clinic was restful and short. The christening brought our friends together. We knew we would soon be leaving Italy. We were already a bit homesick. Our years in Comerio were beginning to blur into one long happy season.

The church bells ringing four times each day reminded us to stop and be grateful. Indeed, Meister Eckhart said that if we have only one prayer, may it be "Thank you."

Off to America

A new chapter was soon to open for us. Pierre was awarded a
fellowship to the Sloane School of Business at Massachusetts
Institute of Technology for the program in management. Not
only did he wish to enlarge the horizons in his career but
together we wished to experience a year with our children
in my country. Euratom facilitated the move. We would
leave Italy in June. Our fifth child, the one born in Lugano,
Switzerland, arrived on time in early April.

We prepared one suitcase for each of us. Our new
mother's helper, the daughter of Austrian friends in the
Teams, arrived from Vienna with her cello. Friends drove
us to the airport. At the other end, my parents were waiting
for us at JFK in New York with a rented U-Haul to take us
"home," a family of seven, a mother's helper and a cello, plus
eight suitcases.

This word home has many meanings. Our home
seemed to be wherever we were living, Italy, Belgium, or
France. Yet Pierre still felt a primary home close to his parents
in the family chalet at Samoëns where he had spent all his
vacations during his school years. I was instead imagining
home as a place I was carrying in my heart, having left my
parents and country ten years earlier. Upon arrival back in
America, I did not expect to feel my roots pulling me back
to where I was born and lived for twenty-five years. Roots
do not disappear. They remain deeply planted. Today we are

discovering that with age they reveal their tenacity and pull still more strongly.

We settled into a comfortable house in Wellesley outside Boston. Pierre's studies at MIT started in July. I found summer programs for the three older children and happily shared taking care of the two younger with our babysitter. My mother had gently suggested that I do some volunteer work. I called up "Share a Hand" and in a few weeks found myself teaching French three afternoons a week to eighth graders in John Jay Junior High School in Roxbury. It was not the safest decision in 1968 when racial tensions were exploding. The students set fire to the school in the winter. There was no heat for a week, no lights, no bells, no clocks. My love of teaching carried me through. I enticed my students with the story of *Le Petit Prince*, letting them imagine that they too—somewhere in this world—had a flower that needed them.

Pierre had his hands full with his studies. He had been working and living in French. Now he was immersed in English. For people who live daily in two languages from an early age, going back and forth comes easily. But for those who learn a second language later in life, it is not easy. We were also now switching to English at home as the children were speaking it at school. More than words were changing, it was also the thought process. We were thinking differently.

It was 1968. Along with the volatile racial situation, protests against the war in Vietnam were multiplying. Pierre and I were listening and catching up with America. It was also an election year. I leaned strongly to the left. Pierre stayed closer to the center. In his program at the Sloan School for senior executives, there were often round tables, discussion groups, and much socializing. Almost all the executives were Republicans. I learned to be quiet. Pierre's centrism was suspicious. All Frenchmen were known to be socialists.

We had joined another Equipe Notre Dame, and here too we learned to be discrete in voicing our opinions whenever the discussions turned political. There were the burnings of the draft cards with activists and priests demonstrating against the Vietnam War. Not all Catholics agreed. Indeed, in our team the other couples did not. We tried to stay focused in our meetings on our spiritual life, but it was not possible to separate our daily life from our spiritual life. Pierre and I never really fit into this American team. We remained visitors for a year.

The three children went to the local grade school. It was a ten-minute walk from our home, along quiet back roads. In the fall it was wonderful fun playing in all the leaves. In winter the snow piled up to our windowsills. Our mother's helper and I took turns with days at home. She had enrolled at Wellesley College. When she went to class, I stayed home. When I went to Roxbury to teach, she stayed home.

The children loved their classes. The school programs were very different to those in Europe. Activities were hands on. There were no individual desks. Instead, the children moved around in the classrooms. For our oldest son Peter, he learned his debating skills as his fifth grade class held an early election. He learned also that his choice did not always win when Nixon won over his choice of Humphrey.

Soon it was time to pack up and return to Europe. Each child had their same one suitcase. Our babysitter had her cello. Pierre and I had each other. Somewhere in our minds, we knew we were saying goodbye to America. We were realizing that as a couple we managed better in Europe, be it in France, Belgium, or Italy. Not only did we work together better but we lived together better. Pierre needed the cultures and traditions of the old continent to be at ease, to be himself. This was the person I had fallen in love with. I not only understood his preference, but I was comfortable with it. I appreciated the quieter, more reserved way of life in Europe than the life I saw in the States.

We were especially more comfortable in a neutral country, as in Belgium or Italy. In France, I often found myself blaming Pierre for something I did not like. Likewise, Pierre would blame me for something in America. We needed to find, nourish, and protect our own lifestyle, not French, not American, but something in between. We found this more easily in neutral territory, outside of our home countries.

Indeed, my childhood magnets were having trouble attracting each other in the States. The little terriers were no longer comfortable in their playpens. Nor were they comfortable with each other. Indeed, they were beginning to scrap. We were ready to return to Europe.

Settling in Switzerland

Once back in Europe, where would we settle? We had choices. Pierre could continue to work for the European Commission which would keep us in Italy or take us back to Brussels. Or he could change his direction and accept a teaching job at a business school in Paris. The prospect of something new appealed to him although teaching was unfamiliar to him. I thought his workdays would be calmer in academia, that he would have more time for the family. He was ready to try. We were able to leave the children with his parents at the chalet in Samoëns and drive to Paris for a few days. Pierre visited the business school at Jouy-en-Josas where he would teach, and I hunted for an apartment. We both were happy with what we found, and back we drove, looking forward to a new life in Paris.

It was then that Pierre heard from the newly appointed European Director of Digital Equipment. DEC was opening its European headquarters in Geneva. The new director was offering Pierre the job as finance director. Pierre had loved all his classes in finance, both at Columbia and at MIT. Here was the right job for him. Goodbye to the professorship and goodbye to the apartment. Goodbye to Paris.

It was now August. Pierre started to work with the small team of DEC engineers to set up their new headquarters. And I started anew to look for an apartment this time in Geneva. The schools would be opening in a few weeks. Our children were Italian raised, meaning they were not very well disciplined. Swiss children learned to stand in line from birth. I walked the streets of Geneva with four lively kids, the fifth in a pushcart, looking for real estate agents. The said agents shook their heads when they saw us and claimed there were no available apartments large enough. Finally, we settled on a two-bedroom apartment in a brand new building near the airport. Three kids in one bedroom, two in the other, and parents in the dining room. There was still scaffolding front and back. The construction workers were Italian. "Ciao ciao, bambini…" We were back home.

We had moved five times in ten years, changing countries four times and language three times. Pierre and I seemed to thrive with each new experience. We were both headstrong and confident. We would make our relationship work wherever we were living. We were, however, concerned for our children, all the more so as we were mixing the languages at home. They grew up completely bilingual. Despite warnings from learned pediatricians and educators, they do not seem to have suffered from the mixture.

Pierre and I continued to find satisfying and adequate compromises in our relationship. Our chosen way of sit-downs and couple dates, relating side by side, continued, but it was not always evident nor easy. As we looked for schools, choosing between public schools in Switzerland or across the border in France, we differed. Our oldest was finishing primary school, so the choice involved secondary school. Pierre thought French secondary school and the French

Baccalaureate were better than Swiss secondary school and the Swiss Maturité.

I was not sure. We worked our way to a decision, weighing the pros and cons. Recognizing that he had the experience of the French system, and that I had no experience of either system, we decided for the French. So off to Ferney Voltaire, across the border, went Peter, our oldest, to 6th grade. It was a fifteen minute drive, when there was no delay at the border. Soon he was doing it on his moped.

All the children followed, going to grade school in Switzerland and secondary school in France. I became involved in the French parents' association, Cornec, a leftist-leaning union. The first assembly of parents resembled a soccer match, so adamant and engaged were the parents on both sides of the political pendulum. It was a far stretch from what I imagined could be a PTA meeting in the States. I wanted the pendulum to rest in the middle. My commitment became almost a part time job as the lycée encountered a realm of difficulties. Finally, we moved to France to make it more coherent. But I am skipping ahead. First, we were to settle in Switzerland.

The apartment was on the fourth floor of a seven-floor building. With its two bedrooms it was not planned for a family of seven. It was our first—and only only—experience of living in an apartment. We wanted it to be a friendly one. So very soon after moving in, we gave a housewarming for the entire building. The children put invitations in all the mailboxes. Everyone came. But only one couple of the eight returned the favor. They too were foreigners, Dutch and Belgian. Swiss apartment dwellers in Geneva were not accustomed to meeting their neighbors, nor did they seem to want to meet them.

Soon we were looking for a house. We were happy with the location in Grand Saconnex. The planes at the airport did not bother us. And France with its lycée was just around the corner and over the border. Our real estate agent this time had a house waiting for us, four bedrooms instead of two, a large yard and a wonderful old cherry tree. We turned the wine cellar into a guest room, the garage into a playroom with a ping pong table, put up a wooden swing on the biggest branch of the cherry tree, and were ready just on time to welcome my parents from New York.

It was their fourth trip to Europe. Visiting us took them first to southern France where they met their first European grandchild, then Belgium where they met two more grandchildren, then Italy and one more, and now Switzerland. We saw one another only every two years. They came to Europe every four years, and we went to America every four years. I missed seeing them more often. But they brought me up to be independent, and when the time came, they blessed my move to Europe. They had only two daughters, and one of them chose to live on the other side of the ocean. Americans do move more easily than Europeans. But usually not across an ocean.

After Dad's retirement, my parents left our home in Briarcliff Manor, New York to go to Phoenix, Arizona, to live in Del Webb's retirement community called Sun City. It was another life. One had to be over fifty-five to live there. The residents were isolated from one another in individual small, similar houses. Children could use the swimming pool only at lunchtime. It was not the ideal place for grandchildren. In afterthought I realize I did not give an American home to our children. It would have been different if our trips to America had taken us back every four years to our old house in Briarcliff Manor, New York, rather than to Sun City, Arizona.

During those first twenty-five years of marriage, I was immersed in my French-speaking life. The Susan of America had become the Susie of France. As I wrote earlier, I picked up the name Susie upon arrival at Grenoble University and the name stuck with me. Totally immersed in the life of a French woman, mother of five, I did not pay attention. We knew very few Americans and practically no American families. When five years later, and all five of our children were at the lycée, an American family arrived, or rather when four American boys arrived at the Lycée, I perked up, as did our three daughters. We became fast and lasting friends with the parents, but the affinity between our children did not outlast their return to the States.

Pierre and I saw Switzerland as a neutral home for us, a congenial compromise between France and America. After ten happy years, we both became Swiss citizens, vowing our loyalty to this country of mountains, lakes, and hands-on democracy with frequent referendums and elections. In front of the United Nations building, there is an immense chair with one of the four legs broken, a symbol for the disaster of land mines. I see it as a still larger symbol for broken peace. Geneva represents this goal of a just world.

Pierre enjoyed his new job, setting in place the European headquarters for his computer company. I again found part-time teaching in the local grade school. Our two older children were now at the lycée across the border in Ferney Voltaire, a small village where in the eighteenth-century Voltaire lived when he left Geneva. Our two younger children were at the local Swiss school, a ten minute walk from our house. This left one at home. Activities were in place, scouts for the boys, dance for the girls, piano for everyone.

We had again hunted down the Teams of Our Lady and asked to join one. Unfortunately, our Swiss team was not doing well. Our presence only added more disruption. The team soon fell apart. We started a prayer group in our home with two of the Team couples and asked our Dominican priest, Father Kaelin, who had welcomed me into the Catholic Church, to be our chaplain. Once a month friends came to our home for an evening of prayer. We had a link to the Catholic Charismatic Movement in the States. Sometimes people would call asking if we would be speaking in tongues. I would reply that hopefully we would be speaking in our hearts. The group soon grew too large for our living room. We helped to relocate downtown close to the University and passed the leadership to another couple more engaged in the Charismatic Movement.

It was in the early 1970's. There was the war in Vietnam. There were children suffering, many without families and homes. Pierre and I started to think about welcoming one of them. We had room for one more child in our family. We reached out to a distant aunt of Pierre's, a

Benedictine sister, living in Saigon and asked if she knew of a child who needed a family. By return mail, a photo of our soon to be son, standing up and holding on to a small wicker chair, fell out of the envelope.

Our Youngest at Phu My Hospice, Saigon, 1973

I have written about Daniel's arrival in Geneva in my book titled *Footsteps, In Love with a Frenchman.* At the airport upon arrival, he fell down, hitting his head on the tile floor. Then he hit his head again twice on purpose. He was terrified, lost, flown out of his country, out of everything he knew. In writing the story, I wrote that the little straw chair stayed in Saigon. Daniel had nothing to hold on to. It would take weeks before he could stand alone without holding on to one of our hands. And it would take years—and then some— for us to realize the depth of his loss.

We were now complete with our six children. The world map on the wall in the kitchen was a reality. We were one world, a small world for sure, but one reaching from America to France, from Switzerland to Vietnam. In the lifeline of our relationship, we were moving into summer. The springtime—falling in love, creating a family, finding our way—was coming to a close. It was time to blossom.

SUMMER
Love's Growth

Together at Daughter's Wedding, Geneva, 1989

The Priory

Our family was growing up. It was the summertime of our relationship. I see the seasons both as a cycle for each year and as a cycle for the life of our marriage. When seeing them as a cycle each year, winter seems less final. Spring is around the corner. We have trust and hope in the ongoing cycle. So may it be now that we know death is near. We do not know what spring will bring, what death will bring, but trusting the seasons—the cyclical and interconnected nature of life—brings serenity. There is a Vietnamese proverb, *Lá rung vé côi,* "Leaves fall back to their roots."

Summer is the season of growth. What is planted in the spring blossoms. Three of our children were at the Lycée. Staying abreast of teenagers in an unfamiliar school environment was difficult. Pierre's attention was fully focused on his job and the expansion of his computer company. As I wanted to understand French schooling, I became active in the parents' association. When the lycée was asking to be accredited as international. I stepped into the association's leadership. The Lycée would become the second International Lycée in France.

The lycées in France are strictly run by the Department of Education in Paris which is unfortunately and constantly understaffed and underfunded, with one reform in place after another. At Ferney we were missing both teachers and classrooms. We parents joined hands with the teachers and students to exert pressure on the administration in Paris. We initiated sit-downs and marches into town, living up to the legacy of the free thinker Voltaire whose statue was in the middle of the town. For several years the atmosphere was volatile. Classes were being held in the hallways and sometimes just not held. Finally, four prefabricated classrooms arrived on trucks from Paris. They were put in place overnight. Voltaire would have approved, except there was no plumbing or suitable foundation. Soon frogs were starting to croak and interrupt the classes.

At the same time, marijuana and hashish were making inroads into the student body. The proximity of Geneva made it easier for drug dealers to arrive and then disappear back over the border. Professors turned to parents for help. Parents turned to professors. Our oldest son was soon to graduate. Peter confronted the hippies and drugs by painting graffiti on a construction wall near Voltaire's statue in the middle of Ferney. « *Baba cool, toujours plus mauve, toujours plus triste, buvez donc du Kiravi.* » "Hippies, ever more purple, ever more sad, drink instead Kiravi." Kiravi was a popular French red wine. He and his classmates wanted to counteract the use of marijuana. Emboldened by the exercise, there would soon be more graffiti.

The lycée was accorded its international ranking in 1978. To celebrate the new title, there was an International School Fair. The morning of the fair, pink flowers appeared on the front wall of the school. The Provisor threatened to call off the entire fair. Our parents' association found a painter in town willing to white out the flowers. By noon, the wall was clean. The celebration took place. When I drove home, I discovered in our garage a bucket of pink paint and several brushes. Our son had not been alone.

The center of our family life had shifted to France. It was time to move once again. Instead of our children driving off each morning on their mopeds across the border to France, Pierre was ready to do the commute to his computer company in the opposite direction. We rented out our house in Geneva and moved into an old stone priory in the hamlet of Magny outside Ferney Voltaire dating back to 1594, the date carved into the massive oak beam in the master bedroom. Monks had lived there for centuries. It was rumored that they dug a tunnel from their priory to the ancient Romanesque church close by. Our children kept looking for its trace.

There was an immense fireplace in the middle room on the ground floor where we kept a fire going through the long winter months. The living room had black and white tiled flooring. Upstairs there were four large bedrooms: the master bedroom plus three chapter rooms. Still higher was a full attic where the owner stored all the furnishings of the house. The courtyard had a small fountain with a stone basin, and in the back yard or rather meadow, an ancient winepress was still in place. It was all very French, and I was soon enjoying the role of a French chatelaine.

We loved the house. There was ample room for everyone including Junon, our faithful collie, two cats, and two barbary chickens who stayed in the tree in the courtyard. We made up stories about the monks, about the hidden tunnel to the church, also about the mother of the present owner of the priory. Widowed, hoping always her husband would come back, she had mysteriously died in the master bedroom. We imagined that her ghost lived in the attic.

Indeed, there reigned in the middle of the large attic a dining table with silver candle sticks as if waiting to welcome her dead husband. One night hearing footsteps upstairs, our children were so terrified that we had to open the trap door, pull down the folding ladder and climb up to make certain there was no one. The table still reigned. In the morning with clearer thinking we blamed the pigeons.

Now four of the children were at the lycée. Soon the oldest would go off to medical school in Besançon on the other side of the Jura mountains. There were now foreign language programs for the different countries of the early European Union. Our children were enrolled in the English program. They followed the full French syllabus plus five hours of English language courses in literature and history. It was a demanding school program and prepared them for the European Baccalaureate.

All the children were involved in the parish church. The curé welcomed the teenagers, letting them bring their guitars to enliven the services. Peter, our oldest, played the small church organ, surrounded by a group of friends, one with a guitar, another with a clarinet. Then the next, Cécile, our oldest daughter, took his place, with a younger edition of the group of friends. Then the next, until it was number four's turn. The curé changed his mind. He no longer appreciated the youthful energy and noise, and told them all to leave. The church emptied not only of the noisy restless teenagers but also of their parents and many of the parishioners. Our children never again found the same atmosphere within the walls of a church.

Since we enjoyed living in France, we decided to build a house rather than to keep renting one. It was on a hill overlooking the lake and Geneva in the village of Prevessin. We designed it so that the view of Mont Blanc greeted the visitor at the front door, through the hall and living room with French doors opening to the back yard, all the way beyond the lake of Geneva to the Alps. There was a den with the piano and a garage with room for mopeds and bicycles. Upstairs there were five spacious bedrooms with closet space separating them.

With hindsight, our adventurous spirit had over-stepped. It was a new, large, beautiful house but we did not need a new, large, beautiful house. We were both overstretched. For me the glitter of a French chatelaine was wearing off. For Pierre, it was a difficult moment professionally. We needed a break. The children stayed with friends, and we took off for a long weekend in the Drome, three hours south of Geneva. We drove down through a blinding snowstorm to a small, hidden hotel, an old stagecoach resting place. A wood fire glowing in a large open fireplace warmed our cold bodies and our cold hearts. It would be one of those blessed moments. A coming back together, a long sit-down, an important *coniunctio*. Pierre regained his easy smile. We both realized we wanted to slow down.

I was overly invested in the parents' association. We had set up a drop-in center for students dealing with drugs. We welcomed them, answered questions, handed out information. A trained therapist came three afternoons a week for counseling. One of the parents was there every afternoon. Often a professor quickly visited to help. It felt very much like a losing crusade by moments. There was a cruel winter when two of the students took their lives. We were worried that a third would follow and then another. A contagion. The tide shifted as the older students graduated, and the younger students were not following in their footsteps.

During these years, our youngest was having trouble at school. Teachers told us he had to calm down. The strict traditional French schooling was not working for him. He couldn't sit still. The days were long with little recreation. And the daily dictées were a nightmare. I tried to help by taking him to soccer practice, looking for something physical. But it only added to his already long school days.

Finally Pierre and I were both ready to simplify our lives, to stop living in two countries and move back to our smaller house in Grand Saconnex. The people renting our house were leaving. It was ours again with the old cherry tree and the swing set in the front yard. We were to stay this time for close to twenty years, until developers tore down our house to build an apartment building. But the old house at 14 chemin Attenville stands in our memories. I see all our children on the swings and trapeze, their friends too. I kept trusting it would support all of them.

Finding a Balance

We were back in our old house in Switzerland, listening to the echoes of our children when the house was full. Our oldest child was now in medical school in Besançon, France. The next was at university in Paris. The third child was finishing university in Geneva. The fourth was at university in Lausanne. This left just our two youngest children with us at home.

The fifth child was in a dance program at the Conservatoire for future professional dancers. At the same time, she followed the French school program by correspondence. She would study in the morning, dance in the afternoon, and want to go out in the evening. Her friends did not have school the next morning. This led to frequent confrontations between mother and daughter. But she succeeded in both programs, passed her Baccalaureat and went off to dance in Paris.

The sixth, our youngest, was having an easier time at school in a more relaxed environment at the International School at La Châtaigneraie in Geneva. He was an ace at sports and on the ski team until his shorter leg from early polio slowed him down. He was soon to finish middle school, heading toward an apprenticeship. It is at this stage where in Switzerland, the children continue on to high school or go into a trade school or apprenticeship.

With more time on my hands, I was ready to turn back to my love of writing. To give myself a boost, for my 50th birthday, I looked for a writing workshop. Hoping I could brush up my mother tongue, I turned to the States. I chose a two-week workshop at Hofstra University in New York, so as to be close to my mother who was grieving my father's death. A melanoma took his life in a few months. He was turning eighty. Fortunately I was able to be with him for a week's visit just before his death. Until his last days he was the calm wonderful father still encouraging me in all I was doing. Ever since he held my hand to the end of the diving board at the pool in Briarcliff Manor and told me to dive, he would say, "Go do it."

For my two week workshop, I sent ahead a story I wrote about a water jug which I bought at the monastery in the Voirons mountains across the border in the French Alps. The nuns there made earthenware pottery. Often when I went for a day of quiet, I would buy a dish or a bowl. My story caught the teacher's attention. It was about a crack in the water jug that I had bought at their small gift shop.

Driving home that day, I turned over twice in the car, narrowly missing the side of the road overlooking the lake. I was alright but the car was finished. I picked up my water jug still wrapped in a single sheet of newspaper and went to lie down the safe side of the road. An ambulance took me and the jug to the hospital in Geneva. We were both well.

With time a crack appeared on the surface of the jug. I wrote that the jug was vulnerable. That the crack was inside the jug. It needed the accident to become visible. It was a lesson for me. I too was vulnerable. I too needed to be cracked open. My teacher was the blind writer Robert Russell. He knew about vulnerability.

The Water Jug with Its Crack

Years later, in 1992, Leonard Cohen would compose the song "Anthem," with the lyrics, "There's a crack, a crack in everything / that's how the light gets in." I was to learn that I too would have a crack. That in falling down the steps of our house in Grand Saconnex, I would 'crack' my shoulder. The injury was such that it could not be mended. It was before micro-surgery. Doctors both in Geneva and New York hesitated to open the shoulder. Therapy helped reduce the pain and gave me back the mobility of my arm. But the crack remains. My Jungian training has taught me to be grateful. My crack continues to let in the light, to bring together my two worlds, the conscious and the unconscious, to guide me on the path toward wholeness.

Writing became not only a mode of expression, of sharing stories, but a way of self-discovery. Through journaling about an experience—about the crack in my shoulder or watering the African violet in our living room —I would uncover its meaning, its truth. I would find an object in nature, something visible, and let it lead me into the invisible world. I remember the white shells I saw one summer day scattered over the sand on the beach. They were beautiful. But when I picked up just one shell and looked at it closely, I saw that its edges were jagged. Water and sand had taken their toll. Yet it was still beautiful. I thought about myself. I too have jagged edges, age and years of raising children have taken their toll. But I can still be beautiful. I wrote about it in my journal, hundreds of little white shells calling to me, moving from the visible world to the invisible, from the small white shell to my own self.

My two weeks in America awakened my English-speaking story writer. I had been living entirely in French in Geneva. I joined the American Women's Club in order to take part in their writers workshop each month. It was a comfortable space to share the stories that were pouring out of me—stories of falling in love, of bringing up five and then six children in France, Belgium, Italy, Switzerland. I would bring a new story almost every month. Soon I was leading the small group. At the same time, I was contributing the stories to AWC's monthly magazine, *The Courier.* I enjoyed working on the magazine, editing the submissions, putting them together. The time I spent on Fridays at the Clubrooms producing and finalizing the pages reminded me of my copyediting days at Macmillan Publishers in New York City thirty years earlier.

My writing career took off quickly. I started to publish the short stories in the *London Financial Times'* monthly magazine, *Resident Abroad.* This led me to become a member of International PEN, the worldwide association of writers working to defend freedom of expression and promote world peace.

Pierre welcomed my burst of creative energy. He found time to be my first reader. He relived the stories of the early years of our marriage. My writing style was unadorned, easily understood. People would name it minimalist, like Raymond Carver. I appreciated the comparison but knew that my style was minimal because I was learning English anew. I had lived and read in French for three decades. It was during the years when the stripped down stories of Ernest Hemingway were also popular. I benefitted from the lopsided comparison.

I was fortunate to receive an invitation as a journalist to visit China in 1986. Pierre was included. For two weeks we traveled in China meeting writers and journalists. I found myself answering questions about the profession of writers in Europe, in the States. It was a very open time for China. People were looking outward, keen to learn from us. We were happy to grasp the hands of the people who gathered around us as soon as they heard us speaking English, full of questions. Three years later, the massacre at Tiananmen Square would abruptly, tragically, end this outreach.

In discovering this other world, we saw it was possible for us to share something from our world. We were both motivated to find ways to give back some of all we had received. Pierre wanted to find ways to orient his professional life to service not only to his company but to his church, his community. I wanted to find ways to contribute my voice— through writing—to those in need of understanding and love.

Our couple dates or sit-downs were helping us keep a balance between our professional lives, our responsibility as parents, and our own relationship. I was keeping notes as we would review the past months and look forward. Pierre turned to our parish and was soon treasurer and then president of the Pastoral Council. It was at the time when our church, the English speaking Catholic Church of Geneva, was setting in place its bylaws. Pierre was well placed to work with both the English and the Swiss clergy.

I moved into the steering committee of the International PEN chapter in Geneva. PEN International was founded in London in 1921 to promote literature and freedom of expression globally. Today there are over 140 Pen Centers around the world. In 1987, I attended as the Suisse Romand delegate the annual International PEN Conference that was held that year in Lugano. The second day, delegates were discussing whether to support Nelson Mandala, the imprisoned South African president. Should we speak out and call for his freedom? I stood up in the assembly and spoke.

Other voices were speaking out, stronger voices, especially those of the American delegation, including Susan Suntag. International PEN voted to actively support Mandala. Three years later the apartheid government released him after serving twenty-seven years in prison.

Our writers workshop at the American Women's Club was ready to publish our first collection of our writing. We titled it *Offshoots, Women Writing in Geneva,* thinking of the offshoots that grow on the sycamore trees along the quais in Geneva. These trees are cut back severely each autumn. Then new shoots appear in the spring, new growth. So it is with expats. We have been uprooted and replanted in our new country. New growth is possible. We can grow stronger branches and reach out further.

Following synchronicity's trail here—meaningful coincidences—a copy of our first *Offshoots* arrived in the hands of the founder and director, Hannelore Hahn, of the International Women's Writing Guild in New York a few months before their summer writing conference. She wrote to invite me to attend. It was in July when Pierre was on vacation. So it was that I crossed the ocean and attended my first IWWG Summer Conference. I felt like Dorothy in the Wizard of Oz, dropped into the middle of over 300 women all speaking English, all wishing to write. The organization exists to empower women, to give us the skills and courage to move forward in the direction of our choice. It has done this for me thirty times over, as each summer for thirty years I have returned to their conference.

Let me describe my first arrival at Skidmore College, upstate New York, where the IWWG was holding the conference. I followed the signs to the registration desk. Someone spotted me. "Are you Susan from Switzerland?" She hugged me roundly. In Switzerland we do not hug strangers, in fact we do not hug. I was overcome and yet something within me responded. Unexpectedly, I felt back home.

When Hannelore asked me to return the following summer, I offered to teach a workshop in writing the personal essay. Many of the short stories I had published in the *London Financial Times*, I had turned into personal essays for the Home Forum page in the *Christian Science Monitor*. I proposed a workshop to show how to do it. This was in 1990. I continued to teach for IWWG not only at their summer conferences, but in New York City, Philadelphia, Chicago. I loved the teaching, the opportunity to encourage others to write. Soon I was teaching also at writers centers, at Grub Street in Boston, Hudson Valley in New York, Bethesda outside Washington DC.

To close this chapter of the summer season of our marriage, I turn to another voyage Pierre and I had in 1991, another fascinating plunge into a foreign culture and country, this time the USSR. I participated in a writers and journalists tour and visit of Russia organized by the American Center of International PEN in NYC. It was possible to bring a partner. We flew to St Petersburg, recently renamed from Leningrad, and met our fellow writers. Each day the program included meetings with local Russian writers and officials, lectures and discussions, visits to museums. It was at the time the USSR was breaking up. Yeltsin had stood on his tank to rally support of the Soviet President Gorbachev's democratic reforms. People were looking for new ways to adapt. Authors, no longer paid by the government, were out on the streets with violin cases open at their feet asking for donations as they read their prose or poetry.

After five days in St. Petersburg, we flew to Odessa, the beautiful Mediterranean like city on the Black Sea. It was late November. Ukraine was voting to leave the USSR and become independent. We spoke with politicians, we lived this extraordinary moment. Today we shudder as Russian bombs fall on the city.

The last days of our tour were in Moscow. I remember the formal final dinner in the large dining hall of our hotel. We were seated with many Russian authors and journalists. The waiters would try to sell us tins of caviar without their Russian counterparts seeing them. Another memory to highlight the contrasts existing in the same one country is our visit outside Moscow at Zagorsk, the oldest Orthodox monastery in Russia. The crowds assembling for the daily Mass, the monks all clad in black, the icons, the incense, the pageantry. Here was a country being reborn while holding fast to life from its past.

Again, as it was after our trip to China, our relationship emerged strengthened and emboldened from this immersion in a different culture. Pierre and I, during our many years together, have been fortunate to travel together a great deal and for visits long enough to speak and exchange with the locals, the residents, across the States, throughout most of

Europe, and then Egypt, Algeria, Cameroon. On to Russia, India, Vietnam, the Philippines. When traveling, we were on our best behavior, appreciating each other and unconsciously courting each other. Keenly interested in the history and culture of the place we were visiting, we asked questions. We answered questions. Both of us wanted to build small bridges of understanding. We returned home more and more committed to contributing to calls for peace and understanding in our world.

Looking Ahead

I was now living sometimes as an American woman, sometimes as a French woman. Which one was I? I wrote an essay that was widely published titled "Metamorphosis," relating how I would wake in the morning and decide how to live my day. Would I be American or French? Even the way I answered the telephone changed, from "Hi, it's Susan. How are you?" to simply a rather austere "Bonjour." It was time to find my true self.

Pierre had delved into transactional analysis. It was again our Dominican priest, Father Kaelin, who suggested to Pierre that he consider a few sessions with a friend of his, a medical doctor who was also trained in transactional analysis. To understand, we both read the book *I'm Okay, You're Okay*. It seemed like a good idea as Pierre was not relating the way he wished to his children nor to his colleagues at work. He needed to rebalance the three sides of his personality: adult, parent, child. For one year he drove to Lausanne for sessions, seeing how he could develop his adult side without being parental. And how he could uncover his more playful, child side.

It was then time for him to spend two months with DEC in the States. While there, his company organized a one-week woods camp for its officers, based on transactional analysis. With his training from Switzerland, Pierre enjoyed the week. Happy to come back home, the 'parent side' had disappeared. He was all adult and playful. So much so that when his transactional doctor saw him, he asked Pierre to join him in monitoring a group of people learning transactional analysis in Geneva. Pierre was flattered but politely declined.

So it would be my turn. It happened that our parish priest in the English language Catholic Church was a fervent Jungian. He was giving a series of lectures on Jungian spirituality. I was intrigued. Jung's answer to the question "Do you believe in God?" on BBC radio spoke to me. "I don't need to believe, I know." His book, *Memories, Dreams, Reflections,* captivated my imagination. Here was someone who also sat on a rock as a child and spoke to "God." He pulled up memories of my big rock on top of a hill behind our house in Briarcliff. I would climb the hill, hoist myself up on top of the rock, and sit there alone to talk with God. The more I read about Jung, the more I wanted to 'know.'

I decided to enter analysis. A Swedish Jungian friend gave me the names of two analysts, a woman and a man, both living in Geneva. I went first to the woman. It was a good experience, friendly. She also had several children. She knew of the monastery where I often went at les Voirons. I thought I could work with her. She would be like a sister or friend.

Then I went to the man. The night before my appointment, I had a dream where I was walking high on a hill overlooking the sea. A man approached from the other direction and pushed me off the path into the water below. I woke up trying to swim in the dark murky water. When the male analyst appeared at the door the next day, he was the man who had pushed me into the water, the same wizened eyes and short beard. I had found my guide.

The synchronicity here astonishes. I still today rest in wonder as I recall the dream. Even knowing, having learned, that such meaningful coincidences exist, I am repeatedly mystified by their occurrence. For three years I went each week, often with a dream, always with an inquisitive spirit, to this man who had pushed me into the water. I name him Keller in my first book, *Looking for Gold*. I had my rock, Pierre, and my basement, Keller.

While I was seeing my analyst, Pierre was encountering a growing hostile environment at work. His boss who had hired him was let go. New people were named. His computer company was being battered by competition and soon would be sold to a rival. Pierre held on for a few more years Then he too was let go. It did not take him long to be called back by his first boss to the European Commission. The door opened for him to return to Brussels. He was ready and willing.

The idea of finishing his working career working for Europe rather than for an American computer company motivated and encouraged him. He would be away from the pressure and marketing concerns of a private company and back to a more easy-going, stress-free atmosphere. He was delighted and ready to accept as soon as possible. I understood his willingness to return to Brussels but did not share it. It was December, soon Christmas time. We gave ourselves a few weeks to welcome our children. celebrate the holidays, and then come to a decision.

My career as a writer and teacher was now well established in Geneva. My experience of teaching in the States had led me to starting the Geneva Writers Group, an international association of writers. Very quickly it took wing, growing from our small group of twelve to thirty, then forty, fifty writers, all expats wanting to write in English. Twenty years later we were over two hundred writers.

The first years of GWG found us meeting in the Café du Soleil, a lively café in Geneva. The patron gave us the upstairs room in return for our staying for lunch. But soon we were too many and moved to the Geneva Press Club where we rented the ground floor. It would be our home for twenty years. One Saturday each month we would fill the large salon, adding more chairs from the basement. We set up the smaller salon as a coffee room, with tables for those who brought picnic lunches. Some of us walked back to the café where we were always welcomed. Pierre joined us in mid-morning to make coffee for the break and stayed through the rest of the day as the coffee maker. He enjoyed the companionship of so many new acquaintances and occasionally picked up his pen and writing.

I was not ready to move to Brussels. We still had our youngest at home. He was now close to twenty years old, without work. The other children were continuing on their own. I was reading *Tough Love*, looking for how to help our son find independence. In his adolescence, he had accepted an apprenticeship in sales. Switzerland has excellent programs for such. But when the school work became too demanding, he did not want to continue. It was his older brother Chris, the piano teacher and composer, who came to his rescue. He helped him build an amplifier and together they set up a music corner in our garage, with a record player. It was music that led him to his first job as a disk jockey in Willi's Bar in downtown Geneva.

There were also our grandchildren living in nearby France. Pierre and I were now blessed with three grandchildren born in the families of our two oldest children. I wrote a story about our oldest grandson born in 1986 who came to stay with us when he was three. His parents were on the other side of the ocean for two weeks. I was hesitant to speak of them afraid he would be sad and cry. "You know Grandmommy," he said at dinner time, "my mommy and daddy are all alone. They must miss me. Can we send them a card?" I would learn from this little fellow. Near the end of his stay, I was pushing him on the old wooden swing in the cherry tree in our front year. "Push me higher, please Grandmommy, push me higher!" When the swing slowed down, he got up, steadied the swing, and reached for my hand, "Your turn, Grandmommy. I'll push you." I love this story, the sunlight on his face. I see it happening. And it is still happening. Our grandchildren are indeed pushing us.

First Grandson on Our Swing, 1989

The following summer there were four new grandchildren. Our hands and hearts overflowed. Three would be christened the same day by our English priest, Father Peter, who had become such a good friend of our family at Jean XXIII, the English speaking Catholic parish in Geneva. The fourth was christened a year later in Fribourg.

Today we have fifteen grandchildren. I never thought about the number of possible grandchildren when we were thinking about having six children. Fifteen is quite normal for six children, two and a half for each. However fifteen are more than we are able to follow as we might wish. We look for those special moments with one or two of them when we build a village with Legos, when we feel their hand holding ours, when we welcome them for an overnight. We rejoice to have so many precious grandchildren.

Back to Christmas time and Pierre's wish to accept the offer to work at the European Commission. Pierre understood that I was not ready to move to Brussels. We talked it through in a couple of sit-downs, listening to each other. One of us must have suggested the compromise first. Might each of us follow our heart's way. Might Pierre go to Brussels? Might I stay in Geneva? Behind us were years of togetherness. Our marriage had a strong foundation. The separation could be a way of honoring our different paths and professions. It was time to accept the experience of living apart. We would come together for a weekend each month, either in Brussels or in Geneva. I think now of Rilke's well-known words "Love consists in this, that two solitudes protect and border and salute each other." (p. 59, *Letters to a Young Poet*)

We were right. The separation deepened our relationship. We saw that our love not only withstood the separation, but was strengthened. Our monthly weekends together were *coniunctios*, bringing together what we had lived during the month. We were discovering each other anew. We were once again courting each other. An added benefit was that living alone led Pierre to discover how to keep house. And gave me the time to finish my first book *Looking for Gold, A Year in Jungian Analysis.*

The summertime of our marriage was ending. What we had planted in the spring had blossomed. We had grown, both of us. So had our children. It was time for the leaves to turn bright red and yellow. And soon time for them to fall. We were entering autumn, the time of love's harvest and also the time of stormy weather.

AUTUMN
Love's Harvest

Together at Daughter's Home, Brooklyn, 2015

Reaping the Fruits

As we moved into the autumn of our relationship, we adapted easily to living separately, pursuing our work and lives during the week and finding one another for the weekend each month. The rhythm suited us. The solid ground of our long marriage gave us support. The separation awakened us to what we loved and missed in each other, letting us forget the squabbles and disagreements.

Pierre, now back in Brussels, was motivated and working to standardize the telecommunications in Europe. He was happy to be back with colleagues dedicated to building a strong, united Europe. He found an apartment close to the buildings of the Commission. At lunch time he walked home for his meal and siesta. His days were orchestrated. He was with good friends from his early days at Euratom. We knew that his retirement was around the corner. These last years were an extra gift at the end of his professional career.

With my first book published, I went on a book tour across the States – New York City, Washington, Chicago, Houston, Palo Alto. I was presenting *Looking for Gold* at bookstores and doing radio interviews and programs. I enjoyed the readings with real people but the radio programs were difficult without seeing who I was speaking to. These last years with Zoom, as long as I can see the faces of my audience, I am at ease. It was only on the radio that I was uncomfortable.

The book speaks of my first year of Jungian analysis, each chapter treating a different dream, each chapter sharing some of the bits of gold I had found. It was an introduction to dreamwork: how to hold on to a dream and listen to it. It's extraordinary how when we pay attention to our dreams, when we write them down, we remember them better. During my years of analysis, I often woke in the middle of the night with a very vivid dream. I would get up to write it down on my computer, easier than holding a pencil. I would close my eyes and the dream would come alive again, taking me back into its world, from the conscious to the unconscious. I dream mostly in English. When I write it down in a semi awake state, I unconsciously mix the languages as I did in my dream

I will share here one of the dreams. It is from the middle of *Looking for Gold*, chapter eight, titled Green Frogs. "I am surrounded by little green frogs, hopping around me happily, maybe ten or fifteen of them. I sit down. There are fewer frogs but they grow bigger. They are now standing on their hind legs, looking at me and still hopping around. I try to catch them. Every time that I get one in my hands, a smaller frog pops out, leaving only the old skin in my hands. I try again, but again the frog hops away, leaving the skin behind. And still I try." (p. 83)

I wondered why on earth was I dreaming about frogs in January. I thought it was a stupid dream. I was reading Goethe's *Faust*. I would not mention this silly dream at my session. But Keller, my analyst, was not impressed with my inflation with Faust. He wanted a dream. I opened my journal and read my silly dream. His face lit up immediately. He looked like one of my frogs, or rather like Mephistopheles.

He explained how frogs represent the unconscious part of my psyche. How in trying to catch one, I was trying to grasp the secrets of the universe.

We turned to Aristophanes' play, *The Frogs*, where Dionysus journeys to the underworld to bring back one of the dead poets. His city is languishing without poetry and song. As he starts on his journey, there is a chorus of frogs leading him. So my frogs were there to lead me into my depths. I didn't need to dissect Faust nor catch one of my frogs. Instead I had only to sit back and watch them. They would show me how to live both on the surface and in the depths, bringing together my consciousness and my unconscious.

I was discovering parts of myself hidden away in my unconscious. The part of myself that wanted to listen to frogs, another part that wanted to be free of constraints, and then the shadow part, the desire to control, the drive to perfection. How to bring them together. All this I was talking about with Keller, my Jungian wizard. Who was I? Not only American or French, but wife or writer, mother or friend. In Jungian thinking, this search is called the path to individuation, the bringing together the different parts of our selves. As we strive to become our full selves, we are striving for wholeness not perfection. Seeing our shadow keeps us humble.

This is the book that today an Iranian translator and publisher is translating into Farsi. She and her husband, a Kurdish Iranian poet, have been invited a few times to the House of Translation in Loorens, Switzerland. It was there that she discovered my work. My first book, *Looking for Gold,* spoke deeply to her, giving her strength and hope that she and the women of Iran—marching on the streets of Tehran—were not alone in their protest. That there is a oneness within humanity, a collective unconscious, linking us together. That my words could reach the women in Iran is both amazing and humbling at the same time.

She wrote to me from Tehran asking if she might translate and publish it. It was one of those astounding gifts from our depths. She and her husband founded their publishing company in Tehran in 2005. We have since met one another here in Geneva. It would be hard to find a more sympathetic couple. She sang for Pierre and me a Persian love poem. Without understanding the words, we understood their appreciation and love for each other. The book hopefully will be published in Farsi later this year.

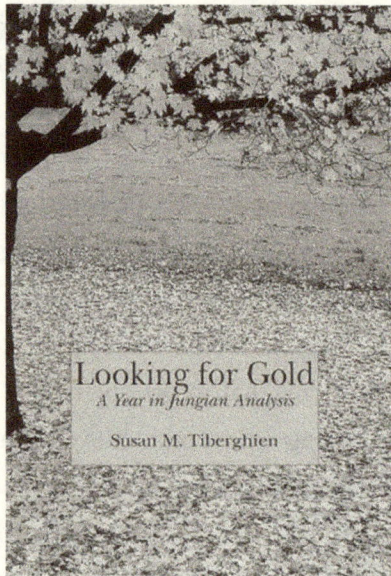

Publisher Daimon Verlag, 1995

Back to the autumn of our marriage. Soon there was a second book tour, combined with my first public lecture at the San Antonio Jung Society. It was titled Tapping Creativity, Looking for Gold. As we tap for gold, we are awakening our creativity. We uncover the stories within us. We become writers, artists, creators. There is a well of stories in our unconscious, but it is blocked by layers of accumulated debris. Once we clear away the rubbish and trash, the stories overflow. Our dreams, both night dreams and day dreams, open the doors to our unconscious. When we write them down in our journals, we harvest their gold buried in our unconscious.

Pierre was with me for this lecture. A gentleman in the audience of over a hundred men and women asked him, "How has your wife's Jungian thinking affected your feelings for her?" Pierre rose to the occasion and took the microphone, "It's made me love her more." For a Frenchman to stand and say this to a crowd of Texans was incredible. It surprised and brought a wave of applause.

Along with the writing, I was finding pleasure and inspiration in the teaching, each month at the Geneva Writers Group and each year in the States for the International Women's Writing Guild. The preparation for each workshop, be it about journaling, finding your voice, or writing short stories deepened my understanding of the subject. I loved the research, the reading, the reflection. Soon I was giving workshops also at several Jungian Centers in the States from Boston to San Antonio, as well as continuing those at different writers' centers along the East Coast.

Pierre, who had now retired from the European Commission and was back home, enjoyed traveling with me. We were discovering together an updated America. Our one year in Boston when Pierre was at MIT was already two decades ago. We had missed out on life in the States for over twenty years. My workshops and our travels gave us the opportunity to catch up and renew contact with friends from years back, friends who still today remain close.

I did not realize how privileged I was to travel this way twice a year not only from Europe to the States, but also around the States, often to cities I did not know. I was motivated and grateful to be able to share the insights and inspiration I was continuing to find through my Jungian studies and my writing. My childhood magnets were happy. The American ones were taking on more weight. It was my path of individuation.

These early years of teaching workshops in the States and returning each summer for the International Women's Writing Guild conferences gave me the experience and the confidence necessary to organize an International Writers Conference in Geneva. With the help of an excellent steering committee and Pierre's financial expertise, we did the first one in 1998. We hired instructors from around Europe and the States, rented the campus at Webster University in Bellevue (almost in our back yard) and limited the number of participants to 150. Two years later we did a second conference for 200 participants. The conferences became biennial, bringing outstanding writers, instructors, agents, and publishers from around the globe to Geneva for the weekend. I had a strong committee but I also had my husband at my side. His organizational skills and finance acumen as well as his easy smile and readiness to help in any way made him an invaluable pillar of the Geneva Writers Conferences. I know it is never too late to thank someone, so I do so here. Dear husband, thank you for all those conferences. Together with our seasoned committee we managed!

Storm

Our lives in neutral Switzerland seemed complete and reached out to the world around us. We welcomed our many children and grandchildren. The house was often full. We welcomed also friends and acquaintances from Pierre's work at the Foundation and from my writing career. All seemed in order until our second daughter, Katie, then thirty five years old, brought a dream to me.

Years earlier, Katie had suffered from anorexia when studying for a year at university in the States. We thought it was the stress of being far from her family along with a drive to perfection instilled in her by her parents. She was unable to continue and returned home. With the help of her doctor and counseling she regained her strength and was able to continue her studies closer to home on this side of the ocean. We have learned since that anorexia is often a result of childhood trauma.

Now in her thirties, married, two children, she was managing a career in marketing and motherhood. In the dream, she saw a man on a staircase in a house on the main road in our village, Grand Saconnex. As she related the dream, she mentioned the number of the house. She was uneasy about the dream, about the man, about the house and the stairs. With a sudden intuition—a prodding from my unconscious—I looked up the Parish House at our Catholic church in the phone book. The number of the street address was identical to the number of the house in her dream.

The dream opened the door to a nightmare. Memories of abuse that had been buried in her unconscious rose to the surface, vague at first then more and more visual and detailed. Something abominable had happened at the parish house. The priest had abused her, the vicar in our parish. She was only eight years old. He was supposedly giving her private catechism lessons to prepare her for her first communion. The dream came to her at the same time that her own eight year old son was preparing his first communion.

She faced the horror. She found poems she had written which she had never understood. Drawings she had made which she had never understood. She turned to therapy, started working with a Jungian analyst. As she re-experienced the abuse, she shared her misery with our Dominican priest, Father Kaelin. Supported and strengthened by her team of support that included also a body therapist and a specialist in trauma in Paris, she decided to report the abuse to the Catholic Diocese in Fribourg.

The vicar who abused her had asked me if he could give her lessons, along with another young girl, to prepare for their first communion. I was myself at that time a catechist in our parish and wondered why he thought it necessary to give added lessons to our daughter. Trustingly I accepted. When I learned of the abuse, I went to the parents of the other girl. They knew nothing about it. Our daughter had gone up and down those stairs alone.

Time and time again, and again the church official in Geneva questioned our daughter. He questioned also Pierre and me individually. A lawyer was often present. The official seemed to acknowledge the crime and to sympathize with us as parents. With Father Kaelin's counsel, our daughter asked for an ecclesiastical trial in Rome. We were confident it would be granted. However when the case had to go to an Appeal trial, the Vatican refused. Cardinal Ratzinger cited the Statues of Limitations that did not exist in the beginning of the trial. More than ten years had passed since the abuse took place. Her case was dismissed, thrown out, erased. Along with how many others?

When I think back to the reassurances of the church official and feel anew his hand on my shoulder in pretended sympathy, I am horrified. It was all pretense. He would report the case in such a way that the vicar would not be judged. The Monseigneur finally got his due and was sentenced to prison, for siphoning money from the archbishop's office. Not only was he perverse in defending one of his own, he was a criminal.

Our daughter, again with Father Kaelin's guidance, then asked for a pastoral trial, meaning with the Swiss hierarchy rather than the Vatican. Our bishop in Fribourg consulted with the other bishops of Switzerland. He came to our house to listen to us, and also to the testimony of a classmate of our daughter. After six long years, the Church finally offered an apology. Our daughter at last felt listened to and started down the long road of healing after twenty-seven years of buried silence and then six long years of asking for justice. Thirty-three years. The scars are deep.

We had let our daughter be abused, injured most intimately, one afternoon each week for close to a month. The vicar gave her orange candies each week. She hid them in the trash mailbox of our apartment building. At her first communion, we watched as he held her hand walking down the aisle of the church, followed by the other children, including the other girl who never was included. Our daughter said nothing, until twenty-eight years later when she brought me the dream.

Why had we seen nothing? How had I, who had chosen to be a stay-at-home mom, not seen something? How had Pierre become so engrossed in his profession that he was sometimes not there for his children? We had come face to face with darkness, with evil. And yet we had not seen it. Only belatedly did we confront it, recognizing our mutual lack of discernment, our failed responsibility. Later in this story of our marriage I will give a response to this question touching upon our own vulnerability. Not only did we ask our daughter to forgive us, we asked each other for forgiveness.

Abuse, dissimulation, secrecy—all of it within the church where Pierre and I, and our children, had felt at home. The impact shattered whatever complacency we had. It shattered our image of the church. I learned that the vicar in Grand Saconnex had been sent to another parish. And then still another. Both of us tried to call attention to the crisis of pedophilia within our new parish. After our year in the States, we had joined the English speaking community at the

Jean XXIII Center. We called for safeguards to be set in place to protect the children. We spoke out publicly, sharing our experience. Regretfully with time there was less interest. The issue became dormant. We withdrew from our active roles in the parish.

I was already questioning my adherence to the institution of the Catholic Church due to its patriarchal structure and its dismissal of the role of women in the church. Now with its refusal to recognize the evil of child abuse within its own ranks, I felt distraught in attending Sunday Mass. Was I condoning an institution that had not only permitted the abuse of our daughter but had closed its eyes? Pierre understood my anguish yet his Catholic roots held firm. We looked for a compromise, a way to come together. Instead of going together to the English-speaking parish each Sunday, Pierre would go to the local parish in French, and I would nourish my faith through quiet prayer at home. This continued up to Covid when Pierre discovered the Sunday Mass on French television. I sometimes stay with him in the beginning of the service and then retreat to my study for my quiet time.

I have skipped ahead here in order to illustrate how *coniunctios* are ongoing in a relationship. Never in the early years of our marriage would I have imagined driving my husband to church, leaving him and going home. But this was the way we found to respect our togetherness Sunday mornings. Most important it was our way of helping each other nourish our individual faith and spiritual life.

A few months later, to honor the decision of the Swiss bishops and express our appreciation to Father Kaelin, we asked him to celebrate a family Mass for us there where he was living as chaplain in the Bethany Monastery located in St. Niklausen, a small village in the middle of Switzerland. The family came together, even those living in the States, to take a step toward the healing of our daughter. It was the last time that our family participated together in a Mass. The damage done to one of us was done to all of us. Each would now find their own spiritual path, the way to an inner source. I call this source God. I learned from Jung that finally it is the simplest and perhaps the easiest word to speak of the transcendent principle in the creation. I see the word God as an image of love. I turn to the First Letter of St. John, "God is love, and he who abides in love abides in God, and God in him." (1 John 4:8). Pierre still has the patriarchal God in his head but is able to treat it as an image.

This story of abuse is a lesson in alchemy. Jung understood the three stages of alchemy – nigredo (the blackening), albedo (the whitening), rubedo (the reddening) – as symbolic representations of the path toward individuation, toward wholeness. He saw the early alchemists as philosophers looking for spiritual healing. The gold was the philosopher's stone, not an external reality but an internal reality. The alchemists in putting base metals into the furnace to turn them into gold, were putting their own darkness into the furnace to transform it into light. Here in the story of abuse, I saw the nigredo stage, going into the alchemical furnace, as the way to blacken the abuse, so as to see it.

Then comes the albedo stage, washing and distilling it, as the way to bring the abuse into the light, to recognize it. And finally I saw the rubedo stage, turning the lead into gold, as the way to integrate the abuse into a new consciousness that included both darkness and light. A new consciousness for our entire family celebrated at the family Mass at the Bethany Monastery.

There would be more gold from this alchemy as our daughter continued to be the alchemist, bringing the darkness to light. Twice she spoke on Swiss television, RTS, denouncing the judicial system of the Roman Catholic Church and encouraging other survivors to come forward, to share their stories. The first time she was not yet ready to share her name nor her face. The second time, fifteen years later, she was ready. She, Catherine Chevron Tiberghien, spoke out, accused the priest, and accused the church.

Settling Back Down

Our lives settled down. The children were moving forward. Their careers were established: a doctor, a professor, a marketing manager, a pianist, a dancer and our youngest a DJ. Interesting how the three older seemed to go on more established paths, and the three younger on lesser trodden paths, ones they were creating. The pianist composing, recording, and teaching. The dancer soon to switch to stage director and to creating a theater company to dedicated to expanding access to theater. Our youngest went from DJ to a job at Protectus security services. His path was difficult. As much as he loved us and we loved him, he often felt cut off from his roots.

Adoption is challenging. Our son came from a different culture, from a war torn zone. Add to that he came into a family of five closely knit children, all high achievers. His siblings welcomed him with open arms. But it was too much to try to keep up with them. He did not pursue his schooling. After several years as a DJ, he became a security officer. And then a chauffeur. He wanted to find his own way. Skipping ahead to today, I sense he feels the most fulfilled as the father of two now adult children. Unfortunately, a few years ago, he had a motorcycle accident, the wheels of his motorcycle caught in the tram rails. He injured his back permanently. His acceptance of life helps him live with pain. He tells me, "That's life, Mom."

Back to the season of autumn, Pierre was now volunteering at the Michelham Foundation for the handicapped worldwide, assisting the president, Lady Michelham. He worked afternoons, evaluating the different requests for financial aid from hospitals, schools, groups, associations from around the world. Soon he was working full days at the Foundation. He became familiar with the world of the handicapped, both adult and children, reviewing the different projects that the Foundation supported and watching over the finances. When it was possible he traveled to the countries to review the projects and give his personal support. For twenty years he gave of his best to assure that the Foundation was serving the needs of the handicapped worldwide.

I was moving ahead with my writing career and published my second book, *Circling to the Center, One Woman's Encounter with Silent Prayer*, with Paulist Press, five years after my first book. I was invited to Louisville, Kentucky, the home of the Thomas Merton Center where I gave a talk about Merton's dark path. Thomas Merton had picked up my second walking stick, the first belonging to CG Jung. The two hit it off well, one supporting my furrowing into psychology, the other my furrowing into spirituality. I often imagine them meeting, each surprised at the ease with which they could exchange their visions and hopes. Merton's last words spoken at an international conference of monks in Bangkok n 1968 were, "Brothers, we are already one." Jung would have nodded.

We visited his Trappist monastery, Gethsemani, where he lived until his death at an interfaith conference in Bangkok. Patrick Hart, Merton's private secretary, welcomed us and accompanied us to Merton's hermitage. I remember the three of us resting on the porch looking out over the scenic hills, the Kentucky knolls, surrounding the monastery. Merton wrote about them in his journals. Here is one citation from May 21, 1963. "The same hills as always but now catching the light in a totally new way, at once very earthly and very ethereal, with delicate cups of shadow and dark ripples and crinkles where I had never seen them, the whole slightly veiled in mist so that it seemed to be a newly discovered continent. A voice in me seemed to be crying, 'Look! Look!'" (p. 206, *The Intimate Merton)* Reading his journals was teaching me to look, to really see.

With the children gone, it was time for us to find a smaller house, hopefully closer to the lake. We were fortunate to find one in a large residence of fifty small houses, row houses in groups of three or four units, spread out in a large, lovely park overlooking the lake in Bellevue, a close suburb to Geneva. From my study window, I see the lake behind the trees and the Alps. Our small backyard is the right size for us. We have a forsythia in the middle of one of the hedges whose bright yellow is the first sign of spring, along with the daffodils closer to our house. A month later blossoms the beautiful lilac which closes the back of our little yard.

Lilac Blossoms in Our Small Backyard, Bellevue

From our bedroom window on the other side of our house, we see the Jura mountains capped with snow all winter. They are lower and older than the Alps. When we lived in Ferney Voltaire across the border in France, we used to ski in the Jura. The slopes were easier and more restful than in the Alps. When planes fly into Geneva, it depends upon the wind whether they fly in from the north or the south. Either way there are mountains on both sides. When the wind is from the north, we see the Swiss flight arriving from NYC at 9:10 in the morning. I wave. We moved here in 2000. Ever since we count our blessings!

The children were now three in Switzerland, two in France, and one in the States as they still are today. We are grateful for their frequent visits and also for our visits in their homes. The distances to Paris and Brooklyn limit the frequency but adds to the enjoyment. We seem to become less Swiss and more French in Paris and certainly less Swiss and more American in Brooklyn. We have straw hats waiting for our visits in Brooklyn. Not sure if the hats are American but it's fun to wear them. Witness the photo to introduce Autumn. Even Pierre looks a bit American.

The youngest of our grandchildren was born in 2004, she is number fifteen! It becomes difficult to remember birthdays. I have a calendar with birthdates in the upstairs hall but I forget to look at it. I rely on Pierre's computer which announces the birthdays. With our breakfast candle we remember each one. The oldest now living in Hangzhou, China, the youngest in Brooklyn, USA.

Pierre and I were now the oldest in our respective families. Both our fathers died when they were in their eighties. Our mothers died in their nineties, both the same year, 2001, both aged 92. First of our four parents to die was my father, at eighty, from a virulent melanoma. My parents were living in Phoenix. Fortunately I was able to go for a long visit a month before his death. We would play cribbage each afternoon. It was my parents' favorite past time. A card game originally from India combining skill and good luck. "Now don't you cheat and let me win," he said, knowing his days were numbered.

Pierre's father was next. It was our turn to be with his parents that weekend in northern France. His father was in the hospital recovering from a slight heart attack. We were sitting close to him, when he stopped breathing. I remember seeing that the air bubbles in his water feeder stopped moving. In fact, they disappeared. We returned to their apartment to find Pierre's mother who was traveling down the path of Alzheimers.

She died six years later in the spring of 2001. Gradually she had lost touch with the life around her. We continued to visit her almost every month. We would look at photos together, always hoping that a smile would come to her lips. We would wheel her into the chapel and sit quietly near the altar. She was no longer speaking. It was a lesson in silent prayer for both of us.

My mother died on 9/11/01. Pierre and I were spending the afternoon at the monastery on the Voiron mountains overlooking Geneva. As the children were growing up. I often went up the mountain for a moment of quiet. Les Monials des Voirons belong to an order created after the Second World War with the vocation to offer hospitality to all. That day I had scheduled a telephone call with my sister to speak to Mom at 4 o'clock PM my time. My sister would be visiting her and would hold the phone close to her ear. I put the coins in the old-fashioned payphone at the monastery, and they all tumbled back. Twice. The third time they stayed. The call went through.

"Susan, do you know what is happening?" my sister asked. "A plane just bombed New York."

It was 10:00 Eastern Standard Time. No one to this day can explain how a call went through from the French Alps to the East Coast in the States at that time. Pierre went to the car to listen to the radio. I was able to say, "I love you Mom." And to hear my mother respond, "And I love you dear." She died an hour later.

Pierre and I were now in our seventies, in good health, happy to be living in Geneva, a neutral home for our bi-cultural marriage. We were at peace with our differences, at bringing our dissimilarities together. Pierre was working in French at the Foundation. I was writing and teaching in English. We continued to mix the languages in our conversations. We mixed them also with our children who were all bilingual. Our friends were—and still are—from different countries and bilingual or trilingual. We appreciated the diversity of languages and nationalities. It was a way to reach out to the world, to listen to its stories, to uncover and celebrate our oneness.

Pierre's assistance at the Foundation was very appreciated. As Lady Michelham's—founder and president—health was declining, he took on more responsibility. It was both challenging and rewarding. The grants were most often for projects related to the handicapped, but often reached out to other needs of the third world. It might be about the penury of fresh water in Burkina Faso and the daily work of the women to assure a supply for their families. Or about la Maison Chance, a home for the orphans and street children in Saigon. I write about these two projects because they were ones that Pierre visited to give his personal support.

I followed my writing path, publishing and teaching. My third book, *Footsteps, A European Album,* brought together the stories of raising six children in four different countries. It went from the story of falling in love with a Frenchman to the story of discovering at age fifty that I wanted to write. It happened that one afternoon when Pierre and I were walking in the Jura mountains. Pierre turned to me and asked what I wanted to do in the future. The question disconcerted me. I was used to thinking about his future, about the future of each of our children, but not about my own future. I was caught off guard and needed to find a place to sit down and rest a moment. The answer surfaced, I wanted to write.

My fourth book followed two years later, titled *One Year to a Writing Life, Twelve Lessons to Deepen Every Writer's Art and Craft.* I was now working with NY agent Susan Schulman. The book was published by Da Capo Books in Boston. It was well acclaimed and translated into Chinese and Korean. I was hoping it would be an 'evergreen' meaning it would stay as a slow bestseller, but the years grew less friendly as the publisher changed three times. The title is now handled by Hachette in Paris.

I continued to teach both in Europe and in the States where I went regularly twice a year to teach workshops both at writers centers and Jungian programs. I was bringing together my love of writing and my love of teaching as I encouraged others to pick up their pens and write their stories. I would suggest that there is always time, to look at how I turned to writing at fifty years old. Pierre was often at my side. He was enjoying the outreach, the new experiences, the new friends.

The first chapter in *One Year to a Writing Life* is titled "Journal Writing." My own journal continued to be the place where I kept learning something new about myself, where I brought the two worlds, the conscious and the unconscious together. In this sense, our journals are *coniunctios*. Marion Woodman writes in her book *Bone, Dying into Life,* that her journal "became a mirror in which I could see and hear my truth resonating in my own daily experience." (p. xi) Our journals mirror our daily lives and in so doing reveal our inner lives. I continue to journal, not every day, maybe only once a week, most often when I feel called to put down on paper an experience, an image, an insight, something precious, that in writing about it, reveals still a deeper part of myself.

I will write about a recent fall I had in our home. I was sitting at my desk, writing. I stood up, or rather I tried to, and my legs twisted and gave way. I fell and broke my foot. I thought it was nothing. But the pain persisted. Slowly in writing, sometimes with my eyes closed as I type blind, I 'saw' that my legs were telling me I was doing too much. They no longer were supporting me. This is the gift of journaling.

The last chapter is titled "Writing the Way Home." I write about active imagination, following the images that call for our attention, actively imagining them, dialoguing with them. Letting them take us within, letting then take us to our center. This is what Jung did in his journals, *The Black Books*, and copied pages of them into *The Red Book.* He would let figures—some known, others unknown—rise from his unconscious and dialogue with them, calling it active imagination. Pierre has listened to me share this practice time and time again. These last years we have started doing active imaginations together. He has his journal, I have mine. We each look for an image that speaks to us, something from a walk, something in our home. We ask the image what it has to tell us. We write down the conversation in the form of a dialogue. Only then, at the end of the exercise, do we share.

Let me give examples. A few years back, during the first year of Covid, Pierre was writing about the wood fire quietly burning in our small fireplace. He asked the wood fire what it had to tell him. It replied, "Keep putting on more wood." The fire was telling my husband to continue building the fire, to put on more wood, to keep it burning. A simple lesson but important at our age. This is the magic of active imagination.

I wrote that same evening about two rather tired roses in the vase on my dining table. They looked wilted, a bit like us. They were leaning in different directions. I wanted them closer together. When I asked why they weren't closer, they said that it was enough that they were in the same vase. They needed the distance between them. I listened. We were in Covid, staying home. We needed some distance between us.

These active imaginations are a way for us, thinking of Rilke, to bow down in front of the uniqueness of the other. We do them individually but together, sitting at the dining table. We look into our own uniqueness. Only then do we share. It is our way home to each other. A way to a harmonious merging of different elements of our psyches. A merging that does not meld the opposites into an indivisible unit. Rather it embraces the differences and gives birth to new growth. Even in our life story, as we approach winter and the last years, there are new buds, new sprouts, promising blossoms. There is always spring.

So it is for our relationship after these active imaginations. We are surprised by the creative imagination of the other. We feel immense respect and love for the other. Somewhere, somehow, our souls have touched. Just as there is the conscious world and the unconscious, so there is the physical world and the spiritual. Our souls are ourselves in the spiritual world. In doing an active imagination together, they have touched. And yes, as Rilke suggested, we bow down before the uniqueness of the other.

WINTER
Mature Love

Together at Port Gitana, Bellevue on Lac Leman, 2022

Baucis and Philemon

"In the hill country of Phrygia there is an oak, growing close beside a linden tree, and a low wall surrounds them both. I have seen the spot myself…" So begins the myth of Philemon and Baucis, written by Ovid in *Metamorphoses*. The book is a Latin narrative poem written in the eighth century chronicling the history of the world until the deification of Julius Caesar, including over two hundred and fifty myths.

Ovid opens his book with "My purpose is to tell of bodies which have been transformed into shapes of a different kind." (p. 29) He is writing about transformation. "I have chosen the story of Baucis and Philemon, a loving elderly couple, who upon death are transformed into a linden tree and an oak tree, growing side by side." (p. 195) It is a love story that Pierre and I wish to be ours.

The myth opens with Jupiter and Mercury, disguised as mortals, looking for somewhere to rest. A thousand homes had remained bolted shut against them. One home, a humble dwelling roofed with thatch, opened its doors. It was the home of Philemon and Baucis, who had grown old and gray in their small modest cottage. By accepting their poverty and living contentedly, they had eased its hardships.

When the heaven dwellers entered the low doorway, they are met with a warm welcome. The old man set down chairs for them, and Baucis threw rough cloths over them. She stirred up the warm ashes on the hearth to heat her one pot. The husband brought in vegetables from the garden. The woman stripped them of their leaves and put them to boil. The old man lifted down a side of smoked bacon from the blackened rafters, cut off a small piece and added it to the bubbling water.

The gods took their places for the meal. Baucis with shaky hands wiped off the table with some stalks of fresh mint and set the table. She placed upon the board wild cherries, endives, radishes, a piece of cheese, all set in clay dishes, and a flagon with beechwood cups. The hearth soon offered the guests piping hot food. The wine of no great age was sent round again. Place was made for a dessert of nuts, figs, wrinkled dates, plums, apples and black grapes just gathered. A shining honey-comb was placed in the very middle of those good things.

As the dinner progressed, in cheerful company and hospitality, the old man and woman saw that the flagon once emptied refilled itself. Seeing this miracle, they were awed and afraid. They begged the gods to forgive their poor meal. Their single goose, whom the couple was getting ready to kill in honour of their divine visitors, kept eluding them. It finally took refuge with the gods who declared it should not be killed.

"We are gods," they said, "and this wicked neighborhood is going to be punished as it richly deserves, but you will be allowed to escape this disaster. All you have to do is to leave your home and climb up the mountainside with us."

The two old people obeyed and, leaning on their sticks, they struggled up the high slope behind the gods.

Close to the top, they turned and saw the rest of their country drowned in marshy waters, with only their home remaining. As they wept for the fate of their neighbors, their old cottage was changed into a temple of marble and gold.

"Tell me, my good old man" said Jupiter, "and you his worthy wife, what would you like from me?"

Philemon and Baucis consulted each other. Then the old man said, "We ask to be your priests, to serve your shrine. And since we have lived happily together all our lives, we pray that death may carry us off together at the same instant."

Their wish was granted. They looked after the temple until one day when, bent with age, they saw each other growing leaves. When the tree tops were starting to cover their faces they exchanged their last words, "Good-bye, my dear one." The trees grew side by side, the trees that were once Philemon and Baucis.

Ovid was writing about transformation. Philemon and Baucis, by their welcoming the Gods, were transformed into everlasting trees standing side by side. It was the couple, the two together, who welcomed Jupiter and Mercury. As Philemon goes to the garden to fetch vegetables, Baucis is heating the pot of water and setting the table. Together they grow aware that their guests are gods. They listen to them and then follow them up the hillside. When granted a wish, they consult together and ask to remain side by side through death and in afterlife.

What draws me to this story is not only their wish to remain together after life, but it is also their loving relationship witnessed by how they welcomed the gods. I have included the myth in the last chapter, the winter of our lives, as Philemon and Baucis were our age. I can picture the two of us bustling together to welcome family and friends. But if gods, disguised as strangers arrived, would we do so? This is my question and my wish. That our love might grow so vibrant, even in our old age, that it manifest itself to all who come to our door.

Marriage, a relationship, needs to continue to grow. I am back to Heraclitus' quotation that you cannot step into the same river twice. Rivers flow forward. They do not remain still. Even in our nineties, Pierre and I need to continue to court one another, to see and nourish the goodness of the other. I could then imagine and hope that after death, we would be transformed in such a way that we could be side by side in the mystery of creation.

Truth and Resilience

On a Saturday morning, one of Pierre's six brothers stopped in for a visit. The three of us were standing in the kitchen glad to be together when he said, "It is not happy what I have to tell you." His direct statement surprised both of us. This was not the habit in the family. "Our daughter was abused by our father." So it was that we learned that Pierre's father was a pedophile.

We were shocked into silence. My first reaction was to put my arms around him. The story spilled out along with tears. The grandfather was dead. Her parents could not confront him, but they could share the story with the family. One by one the father shared the story with each of his six brothers and with his older sister. Of the original ten children, eight remained. The family listened in horror. The father, the patriarch of this French Catholic family, had abused his granddaughter. Some of us believed. Some questioned. Some disbelieved.

We had inherited the chalet where Pierre's parents had spent their vacations in Samoëns. Our own vacation home had been his father's. How could we now cleanse it for our children and grandchildren? Pierre and I decided to banish any bad spirits by burning sage in each of the rooms. The smoke from the sage has cleansing qualities. We recited a short litany and walked through the large chalet, through each floor from the basement to the attic, into each room, carrying our smoking sage.

As we were trying to accept what had happened, it was the turn of our own daughter to come forward. She had a dream pointing her to the year 1974. As a six year old she had spent a week at her grandparents. She was staying with her brother at their grandparents' house in Ambilly close to Geneva. During nap time, it seems the grandfather encouraged the brother to go outside to let his younger sister sleep. The memories were vague but our daughter knew something had happened that should not have happened. She suffered anxiety and distress. She found help from a Jungian analyst close to where she was living in Brooklyn.

I stop here to reflect on how our two daughters found counsel from Jungian analysts. Having myself been in analysis with my Jungian Keller, I wish to be grateful for the listening that Jungians offer. I have found that there is a 'knowing/ unknowing' quality in their therapy, rather than a 'believing/ unbelieving' quality. This, coupled with the attention they give to our dreams, releases and welcomes our stories.

Back to Lucie's story. I had forgotten, perhaps purposely, that I once had left the two children in the care of my parents-in-law. We, her parents, had gone to the States for two weeks. Lucie recovered the proof in my letters dating back to 1974. Then another extraordinary synchronicity happened. Pierre and I were staying in the family chalet at Samoëns. I decided to look for photos from that summer in my parents-in-law's photo albums stored in our basement. I looked through album after album but could not find the one for 1974.

There was still one carton out of place, under the ping pong table. I opened it. There on the very top was the 1974 album. I turned the pages. On the last page were individual photos of Lucie and her brother. How was it possible that I should be looking for a particular album, that it be hidden and that the photos should be on the last page? There are synchronicities pointing us to truth in our lives. We just don't see them.

Even with this specific synchronicity, Pierre and I still today have at times have trouble absorbing what happened. It is so beyond belief that our distress cannot be integrated once and for all. It keeps disappearing and then coming back ready to knock us over anew. For Pierre it pulls up his roots. He is left unsteady, self-doubting, no longer the proud oldest son bearing the name of his father.

For me I am filled with both hatred for this pedophile and pity. I can only think that my father-in-law was cruelly sick, that he was probably himself abused, that incest is transgenerational. The psychological and emotional effects of incest are handed down from one generation to the next without the subsequent generation being aware.

Between the generation of Pierre's father and the generation of our children, there is our own generation. Both Pierre and I experienced trauma in our childhoods. My story dealt with a stranger confronting me with his inflated penis in his hands when I was six or seven. With time I treated it as not important. Pierre's story involved the chaplain of his boarding school who abused him regularly. He had buried the experience, moved on, until something triggered the memory. His psychiatrist said it was not important. We both have carried on as if nothing happened. But we had contributed to creating a vulnerable terrain for the stories of incest to continue. There might be other granddaughters. And perhaps grandsons.

The years passed. For Pierre and me, and for the parents of the other granddaughter, the suffering continued. For the rest of the family, there was confusion and consternation. Then ten years later, a third grand-daughter revealed to her parents vivid memories of what her grandfather did to her. It was in reading the story of a similar family situation, a memoir titled *La Familia Grande,* by Camille Kouchner, that her memories resurfaced. It is easy to look back and say we should have all known. But we did not.

Instead we were blinded by a model of excellence, almost cult-like, by an allegiance to the patriarch. There was a pyramid: the grandparents on the top, their ten children, now eight, the eldest daughter and seven sons, all engineers except the youngest, all married with children, all practicing Catholics. Ten children and thirty-five grandchildren, three of whom, for the present, were abused by the patriarch.

We were immune to it. Immune to the pervasive incestual atmosphere in the family. Who else in our generation among Pierre's brothers and sister-in-law was also a victim of trauma? Who else has contributed to creating a vulnerable terrain? For Pierre and me, is this part of why we were so blind when our daughter was being abused by the vicar? We were a tribe, enjoying vacations together in five chalets, soon six, in Samoëns, gathering together for lunches in the backyards, dinners inside around the dining tables. It was my sister-in-law closest in age and in friendship, a Lacanian psychologist, who first spoke about the incestuous attitude that pervaded the family. In our gatherings, it was as if we were charmed by our shared feigned innocence. We sang off-color songs together when we did the dishes. We laughed when the family sketches turned risqué. We giggled when the grandfather checked on us in bed, on his sons and their wives, to say good night.

I started to see the family in a different light. Unfortunately this sister-in-law has now disappeared into Alzheimer's at a time when we still need her. I felt I could help the family understand. I, the only foreigner in this traditional French family, wanted all of us to come together and recognize the pedophilia of the grandfather. I was often questioned, rebuffed. Pierre supported me when we were with our immediate family. But to speak of it with his brothers was challenging. He finally did so. He was the first in the family to name his father at a family dinner and to speak of what he had done.

Finally when the third granddaughter came forward, her parents took the lead, and they were believed. They asked that the family come together. Slowly it did. The parents composed a document that we could all sign, recognizing the incestual crimes of our father and father-in-law, the deep suffering they occasioned, and asking to be forgiven for not protecting our children. Drafts of the letter went back and forth until it was finalized and signed by everyone, one sister and fifteen brothers and sisters-in-law. Here is the *Document de reconnaissance familiale*.

November 2022

Document of Family Recognition / Responsibility

Since November 2007 several of our daughters and nieces found the force and admirable courage to reveal to us the pedo-criminal acts of our father and father-in-law and the profound trauma that they still today suffer.

It took us a long time to recognize this and accept the reality of these incestual crimes. Today we recognize their reality and the immense suffering they caused our daughters and nieces.

We also recognize that we did not pay attention to our father's and father-in-law's attitude and his distasteful allusions, relying on a family institution where an incestual behavior was unimaginable. We therefore did not protect our children. All of us carry the responsibility.

This document concretizes our will to assume responsibility together for this family history and to welcome further exchanges which might lead us forward.
Signatures:

The document is a tremendous testimony to the strength of our family. It was a remarkable coming together, a *coniunctio* of our vast family, out of which has come new life, a renewal of love and understanding. We now take time to listen to each other. We have suffered and will continue to suffer. We recognize this when we look at each other. There is shared trust in our eyes. No longer do I feel the skepticism that invaded so many of my exchanges with Pierre's brothers. Instead I feel trusted and loved.

Pierre's older sister died shortly after we all signed the document. What happened at her funeral and burial service testified to the renewed creative potential of the family. We were almost complete in the ancient church in Samoëns for a remembrance ceremony. She had asked for a simple service without the Mass. The curé had been forewarned that there was to be no sprinkling of holy water, no elaborate signs of the cross. A simple farewell within the walls of the church where she and so many of the extended family had once worshipped.

Romanesque Church at Samoëns, Haute Savoie

After the service, we followed the priest and the coffin, walking behind, to the village cemetery where we expected to stop at the tomb of my sister-in-law's family where her husband was buried. But the wrong tomb had been opened. The tomb of her parents, the tomb where the grandfather was resting, had been mistakenly opened by the municipality and made ready for the new burial.

The procession stopped in the middle of the cemetery, family and close friends shocked to see the wrong tomb wide open. The priest was at a loss, thinking to proceed and fulfill his duties. Her son spoke. He recognized the mistake of the municipality and reassured the priest. There were muffled whispers. One of her daughters suggested we all hold hands and quietly offer our love and prayers to her mother, our older sister.

Here we were standing all together, close to the grandfather's open tomb and the oldest daughter in a coffin waiting to be buried elsewhere. There was a shared sense of acceptance, almost of amused, affectionate acceptance. Instead of bidding her farewell as her coffin descended into the ground, we bid her farewell there in the middle of the cemetery. The mistake would be—was—corrected.

Pierre is now the oldest. Although previously considered the oldest in the family as he was the male, it is now that he feels the weight of replacing his father. He has taken it upon himself to telephone to one of his brothers each week. He asks how they are doing and relates some of his own news. Last summer we celebrated his 90th birthday in the chalet of the brother and wife whose daughter was the first to come forward and accuse her grand-father of incest. All the brothers and sisters-in-law were present, including two sons of the brother who died. We sat outside near the terrace under a bright blue sky.

Pierre thanked the family—thanked all of us—for coming together. So it was that the oldest son raised his glass to the resilience of the family. Resilience that led us to confront the acts of his father and come together in love to celebrate his birthday. Thank you dear husband.

Growing Old

Today Pierre and I are quite close in the seasons of our long marriage to the end of winter. We forget by moments that we are both now in our nineties. Unconsciously we think, yes we can do that. But no, we can no longer do 'that.' We can no longer go for the long walk we used to do almost each day, along the path "Sans Souci"—so hopefully named— "Without a Worry." The path is not far from our house. It follows a stream from the river, the Versoix, that flows down from the Jura mountains, finding its way to the lake, to Lac Leman.

Chemin Sans Souci, Bellevue

In the middle of the path is a wooden bridge over the branch of the river, le Versoix, flowing down to the lake. We would sit down on a bench close-by to rest and listen to the water streaming over rocks and vegetation. Looking up to the canopy of trees above our heads, to the sky beyond, we would remember that it is the same sky for all of us. That there is a oneness in nature, in the creation. We would continue walking up the path to where the stream disappears under the road. There are wooden steps at the end, without a railing. We had to be careful.

Now instead, we walk around our residence, a tree lined road winding around many of the duplex houses, a twenty minute walk, now a thirty minute walk. Spring is bursting forth, recently planted cherry trees overflow with white blossoms. I go up close to them. I remember a quote from Jung's *Red Book*. Talking to his soul, he writes, "I am your vessel, empty without you but brimming over with you." (p. 145) I see the trees as vessels overflowing with love. I walk still closer and lose myself in their overwhelming beauty.

I will digress here to share what I have learned about beauty. Simone Weil in her book, *Waiting for God*, speaks of beauty as God's trap to catch our attention. She speaks of Persephone who, in stopping to look at a narcissus flower, was abducted by Hades. She became the Queen of the Underworld. I am not suggesting that I will be any queen, but rather that in looking at my cherry trees, I am drawn to the source of their beauty, I am drawn to God, to the source of beauty, to the source of creation.

I continue the digression. Who or what is God for me? I have written about my two walking sticks, CG Jung and Thomas Merton. As I continue to read their work, my experience of God has found words. God is love. I return to St John, "God is love. And he who abides in love, abides in God and God in him." (1 John 4:16) I forgive the 'he' and substitute 'we.' God is the love I have for Pierre, for our children, for our friends. God is the love I wish to radiate to the stranger, the smile and helping hand I wish to give to the woman begging at the entrance to my supermarket.

For Pierre it is more difficult for him to find words to describe how he sees God. He holds to his Catholic roots, his years of instruction, the Apostle's Creed, "I believe in God the Father Almighty, Creator of heaven and earth…" while seeing at the same time that there is a simpler description in the words, God is love.

I speak of the word love in the introduction. I ask what is love? I respond for both of us. "We see our love as the force, the attraction, pulling us together. It is this force, this creative energy, that Pierre and I give to each other. Our love mediates between the two of us, honoring our uniqueness. It mediates also between us and our world, and ultimately between us and our creator." Love as creative energy. God as creative energy. These words echo the thought of Teilhard de Chardin who sees God as the Omega point toward which we are evolving. The words echo also the thought of Henri Bergson who sees God as life's creative force, *l'elan vital,* the thrust driving life forward.

Because of my reading, reflection, and quiet time, I feel at peace with life and death. God—love—is present in all creation. God is present in me, as I am present in God. I imagine the creation as a river. After death my energy will join the river. There is the poem by Khalil Gilbran, "The River Can Not Go Back." The river enters the ocean knowing "It's not about disappearing in the ocean, but of becoming the ocean." Today we are learning the same lesson from quantum physics. We are both particles and waves. The particles will disappear but the waves will continue.

I share my thoughts about death and my trust in life with Pierre. While his faith remains anchored in his childhood, traditionally Roman Catholic, with age he opens to the idea of imagining life as a river flowing forward. We listen to each other and lend support to each other. Each night as we go to sleep we say a short prayer together. We choose between prayers in French and prayers in English.

In French we turn most often to St Francois, « Seigneur, fais de moi un instrument de ta paix… » "Lord, make me an instrument of your peace; Where there is hatred, let me sow love…" So meaningful. And the prayer continues in a second part, "Grant that I may not so much seek to be consoled as to console…" As we say the words, we want to console each other. We attune our hearts to one another.

In English we pray the words in St John's letter, "God is love, And we who abide in love, abide in God." Or the Serenity Prayer that I prayed with my mother from her years in Emotions Anonymous, "God, grant me the serenity to accept the things I cannot change, the courage to change the things I can, and wisdom to know the difference."

We need these prayers. Growing old is not easy. We know the words "Growing old is not for sissies." We also know how true they are. I might even be more precise, 'Dying is not easy.' We have been growing old for over a decade or two. Now we are 'dying.' Slowly, surely, parts of us are dying, just as the leaves fall to the ground. When we can imagine these leaves nourishing the roots which give life to the growth above, we rest and sleep more peacefully.

I think again of Marion Woodman's book, *Bone, Dying into Life*. In sharing her journals, she takes the reader through her healing process from uterine cancer and her journey of transformation as she is dying into new life. "I must stay in touch with whatever keeps me focused on the still point—the place of exact harmony in body and psyche. Simplify life to that point where the dance can happen— the dance between consciousness and the unconscious." (p. 237) There is so much in this short citation. It guides me. To simplify. To let the needless parts fall away, so that I rest in the center, there where my conscious self meets my unconscious self, where I approach wholeness.

This is the natural process of growing old. Pierre and I confront it together. To slow down, to simplify, to accept our weaknesses. In our six decades together, we have worked to bring our differences together, to finding the middle ground, the compromises that have nourished our relationship. Surprisingly this has become more difficult these last years. The refrain from Elizabeth Browning, "Grow old along with me, the best is yet to be…" was somewhere in the back of my mind. I was not expecting old age to be such a challenge. Our confrontations have saddened us.

We have found that we are returning more readily to our roots. I am living more and more in my American world, thinking and daydreaming in English. When Pierre enters it, saying something in French, I feel interrupted and am apt to be annoyed. Our different worlds clash. I respond too quickly, often thoughtlessly. It is likewise for Pierre when he is in his French world. We miss our happy, loving recognition that the other is indeed other and has something to offer. We need to remember and nourish it anew.

I have drawn a little diagram of how we meet in the middle. We see a circle for Pierre's world, another for my world, then a bigger circle in the middle, overlapping our separate worlds. It is this larger world that we want to protect in old age. We need to remember that our roots on either side of the Atlantic do touch under the ocean. I think of the concept of the rhizome that Jung writes about in *Memories, Dreams, Reflections*, the word from botany, referring to the interconnected network of roots underlying the collective unconscious. Here is our oneness. I wrote about the rhizome in my recent book, *Writing Toward Wholeness*, how it is a metaphor for "our underlying oneness with all of creation, the rhizome growing underground that never withers." (p.215) Our long marriage will continue to flourish if we live in both our individual worlds and our shared world, if we fill the space between our countries not only with memories of sixty-six years of love, but with memories of new experiences.

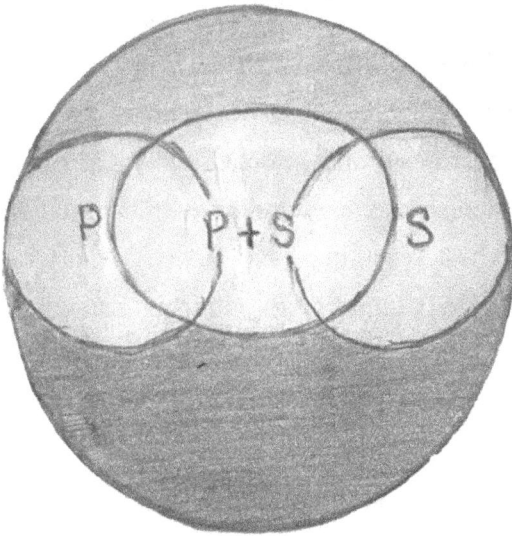

Pattern of Our Marriage

As we look at this drawing, we see the horizontal *coniunctio* of our marriage, the large middle circle that overlaps Pierre's world, P, to the left and Susan's world, S, to the right. In the middle larger circle the P and the S are together, side by side, not fused. We live in our unique worlds and at the same time in our shared together world in the middle. I have added the vertical *coniunctio* of our conscious world, sky blue, on the upper part of the diagram and our unconscious world, an earthy brown, on the bottom part. I see this as the pattern for our marriage.

I interject here my astonishment when I first saw the colors on this photo. I drew my diagram with a pencil on a small piece of white paper. To take the photo, I placed the piece of paper in the light against my computer screen, the colors appeared on their own. I was stunned and grateful.

Pierre and I need to keep filling the middle world with all that we love. With first each other as we are today, with our flaws and our aches. With our growing family, moments with our children, grandchildren, and great grandchildren. With our friends who surround us with happiness and share with us their interests, their experiences. And with what we like to do together, enjoying a good meal, listening to Mozart, singing as we take our daily short walks. "Swing low sweet chariot, coming for to carry me home..." It's this middle world that is carrying us home.

Today there is now Pierre's unforgiving Parkinsons. He does not know from one day to the next where in his body he will be suffering. Unfortunately his lack of balance is every day. He manages it as well as possible. He has a rollator downstairs in our house and another upstairs, an electric chair on the staircase, a cane for inside and ski poles as walking sticks for outside. He exercises as much as possible. On his stationary bicycle in his office, he does sudokus at the same time as he peddles. He goes for a long walk each week with friends, and a short walk with me the other days.

He is helped by his neurologist, a neuropsychologist, two physical therapists (one for land exercises, the other for balneotherapy), two speech therapists (one for his speech, one for his mouth), and our family doctor who watches over his heart and his medications. We set alarms on our cell phones for Madopar, his Parkinson pills, five times a day, and still, we often miss. How grateful we are for this medical care and supervision.

As he copes with his Parkinsons, most of the time I am at his side, either at home or in the car at the steering wheel. The image pops up just now, as I write, for my role as caregiver. A steering wheel. It is quite wonderful when this happens, when in writing a sudden insight arrives. I was referring to being his chauffeur but as often happens surreptitiously one word reveals another. A Parkinsons patient needs a steering wheel.

We are also greatly helped by different programs offered to Parkinsonians here in Geneva. There is an association that holds conferences and round tables. Each year, there is a two month program at the hospital, meeting each week, for a group of Parkinsonians. Here Pierre may do Nordic walking one week, meditation the next, then balneotherapy, and dance another week. The dancing is wonderful to watch. Somehow it enables Pierre to again move rhythmically.

The part of Parkinsons that is the most difficult for both of us is the loss of memory and the slowing down of communication skills, a form of dementia or Alzheimer's that accompanies the vast majority of Parkinsonians who are over 85 years old. He works to exercise his memory: the Sudoku, the game Lumosity on the computer, the piano, a Journal de Bord where he summarizes the previous day. He asks me what he ate for supper. It would maybe be better to write in the evening the same day but he is too tired. He keeps in view on his desk a list of our children and their spouses, our grandchildren and their partners, soon close to forty. Too many for anyone to remember! He has another list of his six brothers and spouses, and another of his close friends. He wants to remember them and stay in touch. As his mother and his maternal grandfather both suffered from Alzheimer's, his forgetfulness worries him.

All of this goes into our shared world in the middle, there where Pierre and I meet not only as husband and wife, but also as patient and caretaker. This is not easy. The role of caretaker does not hold hands with the role of wife, friend, mistress. When I need to ask him to speak more clearly, to stand up straight, to keep a napkin close, this is the caretaker speaking. Let me instead write caregiver. Why 'take,' when I want to 'give'? When I want to love, when he wants to love. Still today, we want to wake in the morning and remember to give thanks for another day of loving.

How do we account for good health or bad health? Why are some of us favored and others not? There is an American Indian custom of inviting a group of people to sit in a circle and asking each person to place his bundle of pains and worries in the middle of the circle. There follows a long moment of silence. Then each person is asked to choose the bundle he wishes to keep, to take home. Everyone chooses back his own bundle. It is a good lesson to understand that we are not alone with our worries. It lessens our anxiety.

My own health is remarkably good. I have had my share of operations and accidents. I am grateful for my healthy body that bore five children and adopted a sixth. There have been three complicated stomach surgeries. I remember being barely conscious after the second one, when Cécile, our oldest daughter, brought her guitar to my room in the hospital to play the classical compositions of Albéniz. She sat quietly near me, played without talking. I went in and out of consciousness. Back to my health, I turned over twice in a car, fell down steps too many times, broke my shoulder, and recently broke my foot simply wanting to stand up. I was sitting at my desk. My legs did not hold. They twisted and collapsed. They were giving me a lesson.

How do we account for our emotional health? Why are some of us optimists and others pessimists? I am grateful to be optimistic. It is a blessing to naturally see the bright side. Pierre is not grateful to be pessimistic. I see him brooding when he is contemplating a difficulty. I see him sitting still, head and shoulders down, bent over, making me think of Rodin's sculpture, *le Penseur.* He sees me sometimes skipping over the difficulty, saying not to worry, things will get better. And sometimes we brood together because some things will not get better.

Recently I had a dream where someone resembling Pierre was close to falling off a precipice. There was a river at the bottom. I woke up. In writing down the dream, I closed my eyes to re-imagine the dream, to enter it. When we re-enter a dream, we can see ourselves as the protagonist. I imagined that it was I falling into the water. I asked my soul what I could do. My soul replied, "Float." The word surprised me. I was not thinking about floating. I was thinking about holding on to something. No, instead I could simply float. And as it is a river, I will float forward.

Pierre's psychologist tells him, *"Lachez prise."* Let go. Live each moment without holding on to whatever occupies you. For example, she explains, think about the exercises you do for your elocution. Don't hold on to them.

Don't make yourself do them every day. Maybe do them every other day. The best exercise is to talk with your wife, family, and friends. How to grow old? "Float," my soul says. "Let go," Pierre's psychologist says. We are trying.

I love my soulful side. It is imaginative not logical. It is not the "I think therefore I am" of Descartes, who propelled us into a dualism, separating body and soul, that for centuries suffocated the spirit. My French husband has heard me too often speak of him. Descartes was an authority for Pierre. Maybe after our sixty plus years together, Descartes is no longer his unerring reference. Mind and body are one. Indeed, as I remind him and as I continue to learn, quantum mechanics is telling us that what we see depends upon us, the seer. The oneness is real.

I asked ChatGPT what I could do as caregiver to my husband with Parkinsons. I received a list of six suggestions, all of them important, and one that I had not thought about, the importance of setting up a routine. I asked again, and this time I got a list of fourteen suggestions, with four that were unrehearsed.

—Break tasks into manageable steps.

—Limit distractions.

—Encourage independence.

—Celebrate achievements.

I shared them with Pierre. I want especially to remember the last two, to encourage him and to praise the smallest accomplishment.

Growing old. We are growing old together. Last night we had friends for dinner. For dessert, I was carrying a bowl of strawberries, a bowl of yogurt, and a bowl of brown sugar to the table. The strawberries started to slide. I tried to stop them. Instead I slid and rolled to the ground, the three bowls still in my hands, hitting hard the back of my head against the antique cupboard behind me. I thought I had broken the cupboard door. Our guests jumped up and rushed to surround me. So many helping hands, so many wise warnings. I know them by heart. Yet still…

So here we are at ninety chasing strawberries on the floor with our guests. I remembered the loving invitation from Elizabeth Browning to her husband and shared it with my husband. "Grow old with me, the best is yet to be." He thought it was the best invitation ever and wrote it down to keep on his desk. May we make it so!

Celebrating

To ensure that "the best is yet to be," we want to celebrate all the good things in our marriage: our love, our anniversaries, our happiness, our children, our grandchildren, our great-grandchildren. In early September we did just that at our double 90th birthdays. We found a lovely small hotel, la Villa Cécile, at the entrance to the medieval village of Yvoire on the French side of Lac Leman. The hotel has twenty-five rooms, we rented twenty-two for the weekend. It was perfect. Perfection is supposed to not happen! So I will write it was close to perfect. An attractive large villa, with an equally attractive annex, a dining room with bay windows overlooking a large terrace and the pool, a sauna downstairs, and comfortable spacious bedrooms with balconies upstairs.

Our daughter Katie and I visited the hotel in early summer. One short visit was enough! Katie took charge and set up the celebration, reenacting her earlier professional life at the Hilton Hotel in Rome. A piano was rented with our musician son Chris in charge. It arrived from Annecy and was set in the middle of the dining and reception rooms where it became the center of activity. Our children grew up all playing the piano. It was part of family life. They have passed on the tradition to their children. All weekend children and grandchildren took turns. Chris arranged for a twelve hand rendition of Ray Charles "Hit the Road, Jack." The six children huddled together over the keys, sometimes even changing places.

There were solos and duets. Piano accompanied guitar and voice, a brother and sister, a saxophone that the oldest grandchild, the one on the swing in the photo in the first chapter of this book, brought along with him from China where he lives. He played Autumn Leaves, while another grandson accompanied him on the piano. I cried. Today I listen to it on a short video and cry anew, tears of gratefulness and bittersweet happiness, knowing the moment is fleeting. "And soon I'll hear old winter's song…"

The children prepared a program for the first night, the grandchildren for the second night. The first night there were mini-videos, *Je me souviendrai toujours*, I will always remember, with each child and grandchild sharing a memory. There was one with children and grandchildren, on vacation in Cape Cod walking to the beach at Dennis. We had rented a large house for the week, with a spacious living area, bedrooms for everyone, a jacuzzi outside, and a short walk to the beach. So many happy memories.

Souvenir: Cape Cod, On the Way to the Beach, 2003

The second night festivities, prepared by our grandchildren, included a sketch "Pierre and Susan at Breakfast." Susan (played by a grandson) is reading C.G. Jung's *The Red Book*. Pierre (played by a granddaughter) is reading the newspaper. They read aloud just enough to see the juxtaposition. Susan finally suggests that Pierre try to hug a tree. She shows him how, as another grandchild plays the tree. The tree responds, hugging her back warmly. Pierre gets up and goes to the tree. The tree does not move.

"You see," he says.

"But did you hug it with love?" asks Susan.

The entertainment was such that we hardly had time to visit the beautiful medieval city of Yvoire, the port where boats arrive regularly from Geneva or from across the lake in Nyon and Lausanne. Old stone houses line the narrow pedestrian streets, inviting cafés, and the large castle, still lived it by descendants of its first owners.

It seemed indeed that the celebration was close to perfect. But then at the closing dinner, our youngest son Daniel, in a brusque movement, threw his shoulder out of place, radiating a sharp pain to his back, causing him to faint. Peter, our oldest and the doctor, took charge. He followed the ambulance to the closest hospital and stayed with Daniel. We continued our celebration while our minds and hearts were with our son. When the good news arrived that the pain had subsided, that x-rays showed nothing broken, and that they were on their way back, it was time to dance. Pierre even remembered how to twist from forty years ago, maybe fifty.

The less happy experiences go along with the happy ones. Each family, each marriage, confronts them. The good and the bad. They manifest the opposites in life. I turn back to Jung, "Seldom or never does marriage develop into an individual relationship smoothly or without crises. There is no birth of consciousness without pain." *(Civilization in Transition)*

A marriage cannot aim for perfection. But it can aim for wholeness. It can bring together the different parts in a *coniunctio*, beginning with the masculine and the feminine. Then the personality types, are we extroverts or introverts, intellectuals or intuitives. Our cultures, our past times. And from coming together, the relationship deepens. The wholeness includes both happy moments and less happy, both light and darkness. I have written about the darkness, the abuse, the incest, the encroaching Parkinsons. About how in aging, we have found ourselves returning to our early roots in separate worlds, how we need to nourish the newer roots. How in the middle of the rhizome, of the network of languages and cultures, we need to keep creating new memories, celebrating our love and togetherness.

Every other year our entire family celebrates Christmas together in the chalet at Samoëns. This past winter it was our family's turn. Pierre and I for the first time sat back and let the children organize everything. The now traditional festivity starts on December 23 with fondues. Recently we added a contest to the evening. Instead of serving the same fondue in five different pots, we serve five different fondues and choose the one we like the most.

Anyone may enter the contest may, but to keep it feasible we limit the entries to five.

The night of the fondue contest, the cooks—the contestants—justle one another as they stir their fondues. In the dining room, at the table, the chairs are pushed back. The cooks align their pots simmering with fondue the length of the tables. We follow one another, walking around the long table, tasting the different fondues, and then lingering near the one we prefer. It was son Chris from Fribourg who won this winter. It's hard to beat a good gruyère from Fribourg!

Several years back, we stopped trying to encourage everyone to trooping off to the midnight service at the church. Instead we created a simple Christmas liturgy to hold in our chalet earlier in the evening. In Europe it is customary to have a miniature creche with Joseph, Mary, the baby Jesus, and a few animals. Our creche is placed on the mantal over the fireplace. Sitting around the fireplace and the creche, Pierre or I say a few words to celebrate the occasion, opening our thoughts to the world around us. Small candles are distributed and lit. Each person places their candle near the creche. As the candles glimmer on the mantel, we give a final prayer of thanksgiving.

We then move to the two dining tables set in a row, to enjoy the traditional American Christmas dinner with turkey, stuffing and cranberry sauce. Here is a fun photo, one year back, of parents, children and grandchildren, all together.

145

Christmas Dinner at Our Chalet in Samoëns, 2023

Once again we added a special intention to our closing prayer. We, who are able to celebrate together in peace, we turned our thoughts to all the places in our world where wars are disrupting family lives, where wars are separating families, and where wars are killing loved ones. We mentioned a few ways to try to help, sharing our own appreciation of Médecins sans Frontières, Doctors without Borders, opening our arms to a world without borders, a world of solidarity.

Celebrations. Moments of shared joy and connection. If I stop and recollect, I could see them happening every day.

When we light our breakfast candle, when we stop on our walk to admire the wild daisies, when we open the door to friends in the evening, when we hug our grandchildren. When we hug one another. I could write that marriage is a celebration. The word comes from the Latin word *celebrare*, which means to honor or to commemorate. Marriage then becomes a way to honor a relationship, to commemorate a relationship. Pierre and I honor and commemorate our relationship every day in celebrating our love.

Serenity

As I close my book, *Seasons of Love*, knowing that Pierre and I are near the end of winter, I turn to the Serenity Prayer. The prayer is attributed to Reinhold Niebur, the American theologian. Its exact origins and wording are not known. It was picked up by Alcoholics Anonymous, the association founded in 1935 by Bill Wilson and Robert Smith. Bill Wilson himself was looking for treatment for his alcoholism and went for counsel to see C.G. Jung. It is written that Jung told him that if someone's guiding spirit remains alcohol, no release from its controlling habit is possible.

I write about this as I experienced my mother's healing not from alcoholism but from depression. Parallel to Alcoholics Anonymous, there is Emotions Anonymous, a sister association set up in 1971 also in the States, to provide support to individuals struggling with mental health issues. My mother was bi-polar, with long periods of depression, necessitating cures of rest. I have very little memory of her absences, my father covered for her. Such was the strength of my father's love. The periods of depression deepened in old age. She was treated with electro-chocks. It was my father who drove her back and forth to the hospital. Soon afterwards she discovered both lithium and Emotions Anonymous.

She became herself again, outgoing, feisty, full of life. Unfortunately my father died before seeing her well. She continued to be faithful to EA. All her life she had looked for some force to believe in. She had looked for God. The 'Higher Power' as defined by the co-founder of Alcoholics Anonymous, Bill Wilson, answered her search. Reportedly it was Jung who wrote to Wilson that the word "God" could be used for the concept of a high power. It allows for both believers and nonbelievers to feel welcomed. That power may be a traditional God, or it may be nature, or the life force.

When I was visiting from Europe, I went with her to her EA meeting a few times. She was then leading her group. She had found her support circle. It was there that I witnessed the power of the Serenity prayer in its effect on the comportment of the members. I started to pray it with my mother every evening during my visits.

Now in our ninth decade, I am praying it with Pierre, thinking about each request. God, grant us
—the serenity to accept the things we cannot change
—the courage to change the things we can
—the wisdom to know the difference.

It sounds so simple but Pierre and I learn each day that it is not. We get wrapped up in our little individual worlds and forget that there is a world in the middle where we meet and love one another. A world where we are serene and accept not only our physical infirmities but also our psychological ones. A world where we remind ourselves how we can be more loveable. A world where we grow each day more grateful for our abiding love.

**God, grant us the serenity to accept the things
we cannot change.**

What are the things we cannot change? We think first of
our failing health. Pierre cannot stop the progression of
Parkinsons and its accompanying loss of memory. But he can
continue to slow down its progression. He can continue to
see his doctors and manage his medicine, to exercise in daily
walks and stationary bicycling, to sharpen his memory and
cognitive skills with games like Sudoku or Lumosity, and in
keeping a daily journal. As his neuropsychologist reminds
him, he can practice letting go. All his life he has been in
control. Brought up as the oldest son, he was taught to be
responsible for his seven brothers. Then he was responsible
for his family, in control of our six children. Now it is time to
sit back, to find serenity.

For me, I cannot guard my agility of body and mind
forever! Physically I can no longer run up and down the
steps. Nor can I do three things at once. I need to slow down,
to stop and think before I rush forward. Even sometimes if it
means saying no to something I want to do for someone else.
To saying no to visiting a friend who is in a nursing home,
to welcoming overnight company, to offering to shop for a
neighbor. I need to accept my frailty, to feel alright about it,
to practice serenity.

What else can we not change? That our second
daughter was abused by a priest. That our third daughter
was abused by her grandfather. That our third son is battling
the demons of adoption. We cannot make it right for our

daughters. The abuse will always be with them. Nor can we make it right for our son. His roots remain in Vietnam where he was traumatized by hunger and war. He was two years old when he was flown away to Switzerland. It is only with our love and our serenity that we can contribute to the well-being of our two daughters and our youngest son.

It is likewise for our other children and for our many grandchildren. We briefly name them at breakfast as we light our candle. It helps us to focus on each one for an instant. To remember those who need extra love. We have a grandchild who has borderline personality disorder. We cannot change this. But in knowing that the butterfly which opens its wings in Geneva, may bring sunshine in New York City, we offer her our love and our confidence in her enduring strength.

We think also of those friends who are suffering from the tribulations of old age and many also from solitude. Today we know very few couples our age who are still both alive. Again, out come the wings of love, the wings of prayers. Out comes also a telephone call, a visit, when possible. We recently went to see a close friend from over fifty years who is widowed and living in an Etablissement Médico Social, a senior residence set in place by the medical structures of Geneva. For part of the afternoon, there was a Sing Along. Pierre and my friend joined voices remembering songs from their youths. They were both happy. It was a beautiful moment. When we give, we receive back double.

What else keeps us concerned, sometimes awake at night, and is beyond our control? I turn here to the situation of our world, the world we are leaving to our children.

Violence and wars. Ukraine, its ongoing destruction, Odessa, the beautiful Mediterranean city which we visited just when it was separating from Russia. And now Israel, Gaza, the holy land torn apart, bombed to dust. Hospitals, schools, shelters all targeted. Today over a million human beings are on the verge of famine. Then my own country, I fear that our growing divisions will create a state of mayhem. We both fear that such a catastrophe would strike not only my country, but also Europe with repercussions around the rest of the world. But my fear, our fear, will only contribute negative energy to our world. Instead we try to remain trusting and hopeful, to send out instead positive energy, to send out our hopes for a more just and peaceful world.

Likewise we sometimes ask ourselves if there will still be life on our planet for generations to come. Will we learn to protect it, to save the glaciers, the ocean coasts, the vegetation in Africa? Again our anxiety only adds to the perils of a ruthless civilization, a capitalism that has forgotten the virtue of empathy, of good will toward others. Instead, I want to be a source of calm. I think of the Rainmaker's story. It is a tale that Richard Wilhelm, a Protestant missionary and German sinologist in China, told to Jung during the years of their friendship.

In China many years ago, a village is suffering from a drought so severe that people and animals are dying. The villagers ask a known Zen master who lives far away in the mountains to come make it rain. He is old yet he consents. When he arrives, instead of performing a ceremony, the master asks the villagers to build a straw hut for him and to give him enough food and drink for five days. On the fourth day clouds arrive and the rain begins to fall. On the fifth day the villagers pull the old man out of the hut and load him down with gifts. He has saved their village.

"How did you make it rain?" they asked.

"I did not make it rain. When I came to you, I myself was out of sorts, like your village. I had to put myself together in order to bring your village together."

The story teaches us that if we put things right inside ourselves, they will straighten themselves and become right outside ourselves. Instead of my agonizing about wars and genocide and hunger, fuming over the stupidities of Trump and his followers, tormenting myself for our planet, I need to sit quietly in the present moment and contribute my calm to the world around me.

To accept what we cannot change. To accept finally our deaths. Not just growing old but dying. There is a practical side of preparation to die and a spiritual side. First the practical side: the finances, the succession, our last wishes, what type of farewell, the burials and I am surely forgetting something. Years ago, we wrote down our wishes in a booklet. Now today we cannot find the booklet. Perhaps it is for the better because we are thinking anew.

We have changed the wishes about our burials. We both still wish to be cremated. But instead of Pierre wishing to have all his ashes in the cemetery at Samoëns, his family home, he now wishes to have half of them in the cemetery here in Bellevue. We adopted Swiss nationality while retaining our original respective nationalities. We have lived in Switzerland for over fifty years and in Bellevue for over twenty. We are at home here. I am grateful for his decision and have joined my wishes to his, resting in a second urn side by side to Pierre in both Samoëns and Bellevue.

Our thoughts for our memorials, rather than funerals, are still being finalized. Pierre wishes to have a service at Jean XXlll, the English speaking Catholic Parish of Geneva, where we became members in 1970 and where he was head of the Administrative Council for many years. He has talked to the parish priest who appreciates Pierre's faith and welcomes his wish to have a service in his parish.

It is complicated for me as I no longer consider myself Catholic. My daughter's abuse, followed by the Church's cover up, along with my growing disapproval of its triumphant paternalism, led me to withdraw from the Church. I consider myself Christian, but I no longer have a traditional faith practice. Instead I find renewal in silent prayer and in nature. Our parish priest would still kindly hold a service for me at John XXIII. Yet I hesitate to invite family and friends to a memorial within the walls of a Church I have left. As an alternative, I have asked the Ecumenical Council, located close to our old home in Grand Saconnex, if they would accept opening their doors to a service in their non-denominational chapel where often we worshipped when we lived in Grand Saconnex. They have responded positively. I leave the final choice to my children.

The practical side of dying with serenity involves also our finances. This has always been Pierre's side of our relationship. He put on paper a complete summary many years ago. We have now updated it and shared it with our children. I am learning to pick up my side as I step in to help. His many years of competent professional work continue to assure us a comfortable life. We are now considering the possibility to make 'living donations' to our children and grandchildren, sharing this way some of our fortune when perhaps they need it the most.

There is also the spiritual side of dying. How are we preparing ourselves for our coming deaths? I return to Marion Woodmans book *Bone, Dying into Life*, "We are all fated to die. Destiny is recognizing the radiance of the soul that loves all of life, Fate is the death we owe to Nature. Destiny is the life we owe to soul." Fate speaks to dying, destiny to living. Fate will call us when it is time. We cannot change that. But we can shape our destiny, our last years. I think anew of Philemon and Baucis. We too want to welcome the unknown visitors at our door, even if they are harbingers of our deaths.

Our years in the Teams, our couple dates or sit-downs, and more recently our practice of active imagination, have given us the opportunity and the words to share our thoughts about the subject of dying. We know our limits. Pierre's faith does not let him stand on the cliff, ready to jump into the water. I hardly dare say that I can do so. Yet for the moment I think I can. My image of life as an ongoing river, lets me imagine that I will somehow become one with the river. As I earlier wrote, after death our bodies, our particles, disappear, but our spirit, our waves, continue to live forward.

A few evenings ago we did an active imagination. Again we sat at the dining table with our journals and pens.

We tried to quiet our busy minds, to let an image from the unconscious emerge onto the screen of our imagination. Once we found an image, or rather an image found us, we wrote it down and spoke to it. We asked it why it came to us. Only after writing down our conversations, did we share.

Pierre's image was the procession he had seen in a recent televised Mass. The interior of the church was glowing with a warm reddish gold light, the priest was walking forward toward the altar followed by the servers and the crowd of parishioners. The image nourished his faith. He can now summon this image when he feels disquiet. He can walk toward the altar.

My image was a small daisy that I had picked in the multitude of wild little daisies at our front door. I had put my single daisy in a vase on our kitchen table. I watched it close at night and open in the morning. It did so regularly. I sensed my soul telling me to do the same, to respect the cycles of the day, to reach outwards with love during the day and then to rest in the night.

We have talked about Exit, the form of assisted suicide that is within the legal framework in Switzerland. In this last year, I have two friends who have left this world with Exit. One of them as she left gave me a gift. I was not present at her death. Her husband related the story. Their son and his two children had come from the States to accompany her. My friend loved to cook and was an excellent chef. She had taken her medicine and was ready to leave this world. As she was giving one of her recipes to her granddaughter, she said "Don't forget the mint." Then she died. These were her last words. "Don't forget the mint." Mint is known for its soothing properties, associated with feelings of freshness and renewal. We have mint growing at our back door. When her husband comes for supper, I give him a sprig of fresh mint. I will not forget the mint.

Pierre has signed into Exit. It means that it will be easier for him to ask for the procedure. I have not signed. I hope that my trust in life, in the way of nature, will carry me through to the other side. We understand each other's choices. And pray together for serenity.

God, grant us the courage to change the things we can.

This second petition is also important. We pray for making it possible to change what we can in our lives. Pierre needs to let go, to be less in control. I need to float, to let the river carry me. This involves simplifying for both of us. To get rid of everything that encumbers our day, that takes our attention away from the essential.

Staying with the essEntial for me means first to make room for my prayer practice even when it feels sterile. "To be still and know that I am God." (Psalm 46:10) To be still and know that God is love. Each morning to rest in love, to rest in God. To remember what I wrote in *Circling to the Center, An Invitation to Silent Prayer.* "The silence of prayer. The prayer of silence. Sitting in God's company. Finding our center and resting there. Finding our temenos, the soft-sounding word that refers to the sacred space in and around the temple in ancient Greece. I draw my space around me and rest in my temenos." (p.18)

To accept the invitation. I know that if I start my day with prayer, what is unimportant will more easily fall away. I will see my single daisy, the petals reaching outwards from the center of love. I will listen to my soul. She is whispering. I have to quiet all the other voices so that I can hear her. My prayer will continue during the day. I will feel my soul at my side.

For Pierre this means to limit the time looking at news and emails, to resist getting caught and trapped by his computer. It means to free his mind, to write in his journal, to go for walks, to play a little piano, to bicycle in his office, and in the evening to listen to Mozart or Schumann. To find a way to practice some quiet time every day. To admit that he can no longer control his surroundings.

We can live our days staying with the essential by filtering out all the noise of the day. Recently I caught myself looking at my iPhone as I was getting ready to go to bed. No. It is evident that the news will not help me sleep. I read in one of Ilia Delio's books, *Making All Things New*, that we have become cyborgs, half human half machine. That young people sleep with their iPhones, only a vibration away from Twitter (or now X). I need to pay attention. We all need to pay attention, to remain masters of our machines and not their servants.

"To change what we can" means also clearing away the excess. It is time to get rid of what we do not need. We recently put a small couch in the cellar for our children or grandchildren. Now we are down to six comfortable places to sit in our living area. Today we rarely have more than four guests at a time. And when we do there are the chairs around the dining table close by. There is more room this way for everyone.

Likewise we can clear away nicknacks, objects, souvenirs. And files, folders, notebooks, and papers. As we clear the spaces, we clear our minds. We are trying to put our offices in order so that what we need is at our fingertips. All this means less care. We can try to imagine our house as a Zen garden.

We can also scale back our daily routines. Letting the parts that are dying fall away. If we no longer feel up to walking for an hour, we can walk for half an hour. If we are no longer up to swimming six lengths at the pool in summer time, we can swim four or even two. When we are too tired to read an hour at night, we can read less and get more sleep. All this is possible if and when we put our both our hearts and minds to it.

And we can accept the help of others, of our children, our neighbors. And of each other. Instead of saying to Pierre, "I can do it," I can accept when he offers. There are so many little things that we can change that add to serenity. When my daughter offers to drive me to the shopping center, I can accept. When my neighbor offers to do a morning errand for me, I can accept. And together we can accept that a loving partner can be also a loving caregiver.

If we look individually at our lives, I can try to have more patience. I know well I am impatient with everyone and now especially with my husband. I am so used to doing everything quickly, from making the bed in the morning, to fixing supper in the evening. I go do it as my father taught me. When it takes Pierre double or triple time, even though I know it is part of Parkinsons and that we are both deeply sorry for this, I still can forget and lose patience. I need courage to slow down myself. Then I will be able to accept that he has slowed down.

Pierre can try to be more of an optimist. Instead of brooding like Rodin's Le Penseur, he can sit back, relax, and smile. Being pessimistic closes one into one's small world of troubles. The shoulders slump. Physically one is exhausted; emotionally one is stressed. Whereas being optimistic opens one to the world around. The head is held high. Physically one is energized; emotionally one is more composed, more open to the world around one. We are all in between, a bit pessimist and a bit optimist. By thinking positively, we can aim toward optimism.

Above all we can remain hopeful. We can remind one another that as long as there is life, there is love. We can see the birds patiently building their nests, one flight with a sprig in the beak, another flight and another sprig, then another. And we know there will be a mother bird soon sitting on her eggs. And then little ones with beaks open. Or we can watch the forsythia bush turn bright gold in the spring, then lose its luster, until the blossoms curl and fall to the ground. We know that they return to the roots. The lessons of nature surround us if we know how to see. Basho, the Japanese Zen monk and poet, wrote that our poetry will arise on its own when we have plunged deep enough into what we are looking at and see something like a hidden light glimmering there.

God, grant us the wisdom to know the difference.

In ancient Greek, wisdom is Sophia. And in the Book of Proverbs, 8:30, Sophia is God's companion. She was at Yahweh's side when he created the earth, the heavens and humankind. She rejoiced in his presence and was filled with delight. Sophia is God's feminine side, the tender counterpart to his power.

I turn to one of my two walking sticks, the Trappist Thomas Merton, and his prose poem *Hagia Sophia*, "There is in all visible things an invisible fecundity, a dimmed light, a hidden wholeness. This mysterious Unity and Integrity is Wisdom, the Mother of all." Merton in the last decade of his life was infused with the love of Sophia. He has taught me to share his love for this hidden wholeness, for this hidden side of God, for what unites all of humanity.

So when each night we pray for wisdom, we are praying for the hidden wholeness, the hidden side of God. We are praying that our love for each other will let us know the difference between what we can change and what we cannot change, that it will let us accept what we cannot change, and change what we can. In loving Pierre, I see and cherish his goodness. This overrides the squabbles and differences. It is the same for Pierre, in his love for me.

I see one example that is important for both of us. I have written about my struggles with being called Susie in my French world. The name stuck with me after my one year at the University of Grenoble. Pierre fell in love with Susie. His family welcomed Susie into their midst. My French friends know me as Susie. But I am not the Susie we know in the States. "If you knew Susie, like I know Susie, Oh! Oh! Oh! What a girl…" In midlife, when I went back to my mother tongue and started to write, study Jung, and teach, I recovered and strengthened the Susan that I was at twenty-one years old, before coming to France. Today when someone calls me Susie, I wonder whom the person is calling. It's not me. And today when Pierre calls me Susie, who is he calling?

He is used to saying Susie. We both understand this. For over six decades he has called me Susie. But I am no longer the Susie he fell in love with at Grenoble, the Susie that he still loves. Thankfully, he loves also the Susan. He loves her differently. The Serenity Prayer has helped us. We pray for the wisdom to know what we can change and what we cannot change and the serenity to accept it. I pray to see the Susie as my husband sees her. Pierre prays to see the Susan as she is today. And together we pray to Sophia that she continue to grace our love with her presence.

I come to the end of this memoir about our long marriage with thanksgiving for our love. I remember always Meister Eckhart's counsel six centuries ago, if we have only one prayer may it be "Thank You." I relive that first kiss at Bellagio, the kiss that I still taste. Our romance began and would grow through the seasons of love.

First spring: we experienced young love, off to southern France, the air force, and soon our first child. To Brussels, a united Europe, and two more children. On to Italy, everything was possible, our love reached out still further with another two more children. A year in America, a full house, and back to Europe, to Switzerland, where we welcomed our sixth.

Summer came. We detoured to France, watched the children grow into early adulthood, looked for our balance, and then returned to Switzerland to our house on chemin Attenville. Time for my writing and for my foray into Jungian psychology. Time for Pierre's professional career in a multinational.

Autumn found us happily handling our two professions, Pierre back in Brussels for Europe, I in Geneva, writing and teaching. Then the story of abuse erupted, only to be thrown five years later into the bin by the Vatican at Rome. The Catholic Church was no longer our welcoming home. The family stood together. Pierre and I settled down in our new home near the lake.

Winter came with old age. It started menacingly with the story of incest. The family— this time the larger family including all of Pierre's siblings and their families — held strong and composed a document of recognition. Pierre's Parkinsons arrived. He manages it as well as possible. We are grateful for these last years together where we wake in our home each morning to welcome a new day of loving.

Together at Yvoire for our Ninetieth Birthdays,
September 2023

May Sophia Wisdom enlighten us with the gifts of serenity and courage. Let us help each other to rest serene and courageous. May we trust the deep cycle of nature where the seasons follow one another and life is renewed, reborn. Let us welcome autumn as we welcome spring, winter as we welcome summer. May we trust the seasons of love. After winter, there will be spring.

Acknowledgments

I would need to start from our first kiss to acknowledge all the hands and hearts who have contributed to *Seasons of Love*.

First and foremost I am grateful to my husband, Pierre-Yves, whose goodness and arms have held me over six decades, who has read this book, page by page, rewrite by rewrite.

To my children who have always stood at me side, to Catherine, my daughter editor and first reader, to Lucie and to Cecile my other daughters, and to my sons Pierre-William, Christopher and Daniel, they taught me trust and resilience.

To our close friends from France, Belgium, Italy, Switzerland, from friends of the Equipes Notre Dame, from Pierre's professional work, from my writing and teaching, from the International Women's Writing Guild, and the Geneva Writers Group. In particular to my close friend Wallis Wilde Menozzi, one of the readers of my book.

With the final acknowledgement to C.G. Jung and to all Jungians who have helped me understand many of his teachings. I think of my analyst Keller and also of my friend and analyst Kristina Schellinski. I think of the many authors whose works I have studied. Of Sonu Shamdasani, who through his translation of *The Red Book* taught me to speak to my soul.

I am grateful to all of you. It is my fervent hope that C.G. Jung, with Thomas Merton, will continue with increasing visibility to show us the way to the victory of light over darkness. "That is the service which man can render to God, that light may emerge from the darkness." (p. 371, *Memories, Dreams, Reflections)*

Index

About the Author

Susan Tiberghien, an American writer living in Geneva, Switzerland, holds a degree in Literature and Philosophy and did graduate work at Grenoble University, France and the CG Jung Institute, Kusnacht, Switzerland.

She has published four memoirs: *Looking for Gold, A Year in Jungian Analysis; Circling to the Center, Invitation to Silent Prayer; Side by Side, Writing Your Love Story; Footsteps, In Love with a Frenchman,* and two writing handbooks: *One Year to a Writing Life, Twelve Lessons to Deepen Every Writer's Art and Craft;* and most recently *Writing Toward Wholeness, Lessons Inspired by CG Jung,* along with numerous essays in journals and anthologies on both sides of the Atlantic.

Tiberghien has been teaching Jungian informed writing workshops for over twenty-five years at CG Jung Societies, at the International Women's Writing Guild, and at writers' centers and conferences in the States and in Europe. Recently she has recorded courses for the Jung Society of Washington DC, for Soul at Play, and for the Jung Platform.

She is an active member of International Pen, a founding member of the International Writers' Residence at Lavigny, Switzerland, the founder and past director of the Geneva Writers' Group, an association of over 240 English-language writers.

Mother of six children, grandmother of fifteen grandchildren, and great grandmother of three great grandchildren, she lives with her French husband in Geneva, Switzerland, a city whose dedication to peace and justice she fully endorses.

www.ingramcontent.com/pod-product-compliance
Lightning Source LLC
Chambersburg PA
CBHW031512270326
41930CB00006B/376